Workshop Facilitation Handbook
A Step-by-Step Approach

Workshop Facilitation Handbook
A Step-by-Step Approach

Rod Baxter

2015

Copyright © 2015 by Rod Baxter
Edited by Kelli Baxter

All rights reserved. This book or any portion thereof may not be reproduced or used in any manner whatsoever without the express written permission of the publisher, except for the use of brief quotations in a book review or scholarly journal.

First Edition: 2015

ISBN 9798359462181

Value Generation Partners, LLC
Naples, Florida 34109

You can follow the author at:
https://www.linkedin.com/in/rodbaxter/

With the purchase of this workbook, you are eligible to receive a complementary MS Excel® file, which contains the templates referenced in these chapters.

To download your complementary toolbox, please visit https://www.linkedin.com/company/value-generation-partners/ and select the Google Drive link.

Check out "Operational Excellence Handbook" by Rod Baxter for more problem-solving and process-improvement tools and techniques.

Contents

Introduction: Workshop Facilitation for Success 1
   The Workshop Facilitator 3

Seven-Step Workshop Facilitation Approach 5
   Step One: Set-up the Workshop Charter 5
      Workshop Charter 6
      SMART Workshop Goal 7
   Step Two: Understand the Logistics 8
   Step Three: Create the Team 9
   Step Four: Clarify Roles and Responsibilities 10
   Step Five: Execute the Workshop 10
   Step Six: Share Status of Workshop 14
   Step Seven: Salute the Team 14

Workshop Facilitator's Toolbox 16
   5 Why Root Cause Analysis 16
   Action Plan 17
   Affinity Diagram 18
   Brainstorming 20
   Cause-and-Effect (C&E) Diagram 21
   Cause-and-Effect (X-Y) Matrix 23
   Communication Plan 25
      Informative Communication 26
      Concise Communications 28
   Conflict Resolution 29
   Consensus Building 31
   Control Plan 33
   Decision Tree 35
   Fault Tree Analysis (FTA) 37
   Force Field Analysis 40
   Failure Modes and Effects Analysis (FMEA) 42
   Impact/Effort Analysis 45
   Mind Mapping 47
   Multivoting 49
   Nominal Group Technique (NGT) 50
   Pairwise Comparison 52
   Process Maps 54
   Pugh Matrix 59
   RACI 61

Contents

SIPOC 63
Six Thinking Hats 65
Solution-Selection Matrix 67
SWOT Analysis 69
Team Building 72
Training Plan 76

Summary: Workshop Facilitation for Success 78

Introduction: Workshop Facilitation for Success

Workshop Facilitation for Success is an efficient and effective approach to managing and achieving goals and objectives in a face-to-face, cross-functional environment. Workshop facilitation (also known as Kaizen events, continuous improvement events, quality improvement events, workout sessions, and process improvement events) may be conducted as one-day to five-day events. Workshops are conducted to achieve goals and objectives based on many purposes, such as process improvement, waste reduction, cost-of-quality reduction, project selection, and strategy development and deployment. Much thought and consideration must be given to planning and conducting workshop facilitation to ensure successful outcomes.

Workshop facilitation may be useful when:

- There are many and varying opinions on how to achieve goals and objectives
- Goals and objectives must be completed in a short cycle time
- Team and cross-functional collaboration are necessary to ensure success of goals and objectives
- It is necessary for a group to work in a face-to-face environment to achieve goals and objectives
- Goals and objectives include waste reduction, cycle-time reduction, process improvement, or quality improvement

This simple seven-step approach, called Workshop Facilitation for Success, may be applied to achieve goals and objectives in any industry – healthcare, construction, manufacturing, service, hospitality, non-profit,

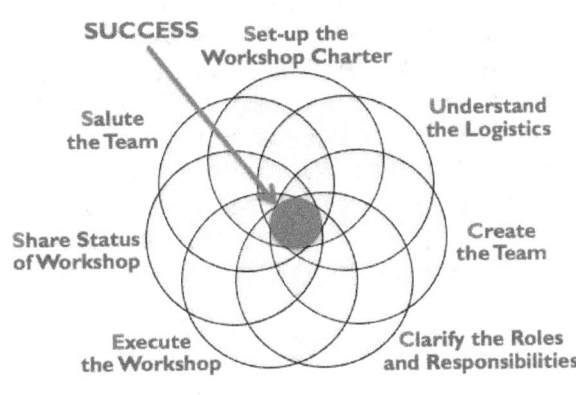

Introduction: Workshop Facilitation for Success

government, financial, etc. Workshop Facilitation for Success is designed for facilitators of all levels, regardless of their role, business, and industry. It combines the most effective and efficient elements of workshop facilitation approaches into the following seven steps:

1. **Set-up the Workshop Charter** – define, develop, and approve a workshop charter that outlines the workshop description, clear goals, deliverables, objectives, in/out of scope, success criteria, and timeline for completion
2. **Understand the Logistics** – determine the workshop budget, where and when it will be conducted, and the duration of the workshop

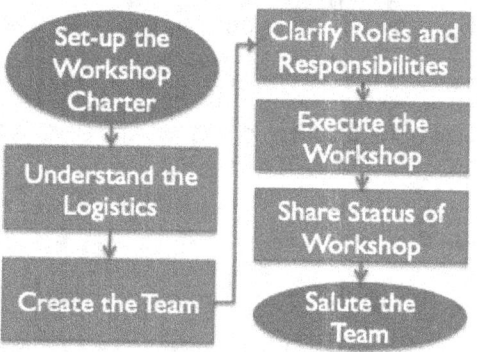

3. **Create the Team** – identify participants and experience required to conduct the workshop and achieve the goals and objectives
4. **Clarify Roles and Responsibilities** – conduct a workshop kick-off call with the participants to describe workshop purpose, goals, and deliverables; roles and responsibilities before, during, and after the workshop; provide participants with pre-work assignments
5. **Execute the Workshop** – conduct the workshop using a defined agenda, along with tools and techniques as described in the Workshop Facilitator's Toolbox section of this handbook, to manage through a full and clear understanding of current-state (as is) condition and defining future-state (to be) condition, along with an executable action plan
6. **Share Status of Workshop** – conduct report-out at the conclusion of the workshop, then conduct ongoing status reporting post workshop until all action items are complete
7. **Salute the Team** – recognize the team and celebrate success

Introduction: Workshop Facilitation for Success

Benefits of workshop facilitation include:

- Provide a collaborative team environment
- Provide a consistent approach for facilitating workshops
- Increase focus and attention on goals and objectives
- Save cost and time through rapid goal and objective achievement
- Provide an efficient and effective approach for achieving goals and objectives

Workshop Facilitation Handbook may be supplemented with the following handbooks based on the goal, objectives, scope, and deliverables of the workshop.

- ***Strategy Deployment Handbook*** if the workshop scope and deliverables include strategic planning, strategy mapping, KPI development, or balanced and cascading scorecards
- ***Project Management Handbook*** if the workshop will lead to the launch of formal projects
- ***Problem Solving Handbook*** if the workshop goal and objectives include the need for root cause analysis and problem solving

We wish you much success in your pursuit of Workshop Facilitation for Success, thereby generating greater organizational value!

The Workshop Facilitator

A workshop facilitator requires a special and specific skillset. From the Tao Te Ching text, "When I give up trying to impress the group, I become very impressive. Let go in order to achieve. The wise facilitator speaks rarely and briefly, teaching more through being than doing." Workshop facilitators are confronted with a wide variation of conditions and pressures. Workshops often bring together a diverse group of individuals who do not normally work together and many times do not have the same goals and performance metrics.

Workshops are disruptive to the participants' daily functions and may require extra work and hours to maintian daily business, along with participating in the workshop. Often workshop particpants are chosen, rather than volunteering to particpate in the workshop. The facilitator must be prepared with a wide variety of tools and techniques to ensure smooth and successful workshops. The section

Introduction: Workshop Facilitation for Success

in this workbook titled, "Workshop Facilitator's Toolbox," is a useful set of tools and techniques to provide for successful workshops.

Qualities and characteristics of an effective workshop facilitator:

1. Has fun and brings fun to the workshop session
2. Is able to manage conflict and build consensus
3. Brings about complete involvement of all workshop participants
4. Manages the workshop agenda with flexibility, while maintaining focus on the goals and objectives
5. Provides for a safe environment where participants are able to express opinions and ideas without fear
6. Is able to guide conversation in a way that brings out innovative ideas from the participants
7. Is masterful at listening and stimulating ideas and interaction
8. Utilizes ground rules to protect the participants
9. Manages to the needs of the individuals as well as the team
10. Takes a neutral position, allowing for the participants to generate the ideas and solutions
11. Recognizes that the participants are the topic or process experts and draws on their expertise
12. Utilizes a variety of tools, techniques, and approaches to engage the participants and achieve the goals and objectives
13. Is honest, sincere, and open with the participants

Workshop Facilitation for Success provides the reader with a seven-step process, along with many tools and techniques for facilitating succesful workshops. For best results, utilize the workshop charter and SMART goal, in conjunction with the seven-step process and Workshop Facilitator's Toolbox, to design and conduct a successful workshop.

Seven-Step Workshop Facilitation Approach

The following chapters make up the seven-step Workshop Facilitation for Success approach.

Step One: Set-up the Workshop Charter
Step Two: Understand the Logistics
Step Three: Create the Team
Step Four: Clarify Roles and Responsibilities
Step Five: Execute the Workshop
Step Six: Share Status of Workshop
Step Seven: Salute the Team

Step One: Set-up the Workshop Charter

Step One of Workshop Facilitation for Success is Set-up the Workshop Charter. The charter is essentially a contract between the workshop facilitator, sponsor, and workshop team by which to execute the workshop according to clearly and concisely defined deliverables, goal, scope, and success criteria. Peter Drucker is credited with the quote, "Unless commitment is made, there are only promises and hopes; but no plans." The workshop charter is the commitment by which the workshop is planned and executed.

Process to Set-up the Workshop Charter:

1. Identify workshop facilitator, sponsor, and key stakeholders
2. Workshop facilitator and sponsor develop workshop charter
    a. Workshop description
    b. SMART goals, objectives, deliverables
    c. Timeline for completion
    d. In-scope and out-of-scope statements
    e. Success criteria, metrics, and KPIs
    f. Issues, risks, dependencies
3. Continue to Step Two: Understand the Logistics

Seven-Step Workshop Facilitation Approach

Workshop Charter

Benefits of a well-documented workshop charter include:

- Detailing the workshop purpose
- Providing alignment of the goals and objectives to the workshop team members
- Securing authority to execute to a plan
- Serving as a reference point to ensure focus on the workshop goals, objectives, and deliverables
- Providing a baseline for changes to goals, objectives, deliverables, and scope
- Describing what success means for the workshop team

This following template works well as a workshop charter.

VALUE GENERATION PARTNERS

Workshop Charter

Workshop Name:		Charter Date:	Identification Number:
Workshop Sponsor:		Workshop Facilitator:	
Impacted Business Department:		Expected Project Cost:	Refined Financial Outcome:

PROJECT DETAIL

WORKSHOP PURPOSE	Problem statement and the benefit statement of the workshop
WORKSHOP GOAL	SMART Goal (Specific - Measurable - Achievable - Relevant - Time-bound)
WORKSHOP SCOPE	In Scope and Out of Scope
SUCCESS CRITERIA	Metrics for Success (Primary and Secondary Metrics)
CONCERNS	Issues, Risks, and Dependencies

CHARTER APPROVALS	Approval Date:	Approved by:

SMART Workshop Goal

Developing a SMART workshop goal is critical to Workshop Facilitation for Success. The use of SMART goals has been credited to Peter Drucker, through his management by objectives concept. The first-known writing of the term "SMART" occurs in the November 1981 issue of Management Review, in George T. Doran's article, "There's a S.M.A.R.T. Way to Write Management's Goals and Objectives."

Benefits of SMART workshop goals include providing:

- Motivation to the workshop team members
- Foundation and base for workshop status updates and reviews
- Clarity regarding workshop goals, objectives, and deliverables
- A collaborative team environment

A discussion about facilitating a workshop would not be complete without talking about SMART goals. Consider the following three goal statements:

1. Shorten emergency room patient wait time
2. Improve software coding errors
3. Reduce our employee turnover rate

What is wrong with the three goals, and how might they be better stated? In each case, we don't know current quality levels, planned improvement levels, and when it will be complete. How might we improve these three workshop goal statements using a SMART goal approach? A goal is considered **SMART** if it is **S**pecific, **M**easurable, **A**chievable, **R**elevant, and **T**ime-Bound.

Define a SMART workshop goal using the template depicted in the following image. Then, test it against the checklist to determine if it passes SMART goal criteria.

Seven-Step Workshop Facilitation Approach

SMART Workshop Goal — VALUE GENERATION PARTNERS

Facilitator:		Date:
Organization and location of goal		
Function and process of goal		
Current quality level of problem		
Desired quality level of goal		
Desired completion date of goal		
SMART Goal Statement:		
Is the goal **Specific**?	Did you describe what process or outcome you plan to increase or decrease?	
Is the goal **Measurable**?	Did you list the current quality level and planned improvement level for when it is complete?	
Is the goal **Achievable**?	Did you base your planned quality level on facts and data?	
Is the goal **Relevant**?	Does your goal support the strategic initiatives of the organization and is it within your scope of influence and responsibility?	
Is the goal **Time-Bound**?	Did you list a date by which to achieve the improvement level?	

Do these three rewritten goals pass the SMART goal criteria?

1. Reduce Hospital General North Campus emergency room patient wait time from 90 minutes to the goal of 30 minutes by June 30 of this calendar year
2. Increase Software by Us coding accuracy for point-of-sales devices in North America from one error for every 10,000 lines of code to the company goal of three coding errors per million lines of code by December 31 of this calendar year
3. Reduce University of Learnings administrative turnover rate from the current 15% per year to the university goal of 3% per year by March 15 of this calendar year

If you cannot answer "yes" to all of the SMART goal questions in the template, continue to define the goal until you can.

Step Two: Understand the Logistics

Step Two of Workshop Facilitation for Success is Understand the Logistics. While it may seem like a very basic and simple step, it is important to understand and manage appropriate logistics in order to ensure participants have everything necessary to focus on the workshop purpose, goals, and deliverables. Understanding and managing the workshop logistics appropriately will support and enable a successful workshop outcome and achievement of the goals, objectives, and deliverables.

Process to Understand the Logistics:

1. Facilitator and sponsor determine workshop budget for travel, location, snacks, lunches, etc.
2. Facilitator and sponsor determine the workshop date, location, and duration; ideally the participants are provided two to four weeks to prepare for the workshop topic and schedule
3. Facilitator secures workshop location and supplies
    a. Butcher block paper, flip charts, Post-it® notes, markers, tape, digital projector, etc.
4. Facilitator plans to arrive at the workshop location in advance to ensure appropriate set-up and preparation
    a. U-shape room arrangement, refreshments (water, coffee, snacks, etc.), event supplies, etc.
5. Continue to Step Three: Create the Team

Step Three: Create the Team

Step Three of Workshop Facilitation for Success is Create the Team. Babe Ruth is quoted as saying, "The way a team plays as a whole determines its success. You may have the greatest bunch of individual stars in the world, but if they don't play together, the club won't be worth a dime." Successfully achieving the workshop goals, objectives, and deliverables is highly dependent on the workshop team. Thought and consideration must be given to selecting a team that can and will work together, resulting in a successful workshop.

Process to Create the Team:

1. Facilitator and sponsor identify workshop participants and expertise required based on workshop goals, objectives, and deliverables
    a. Subject matter experts (SMEs)
    b. Decision-making support
    c. Analytical support
    d. Technical support
    e. Documentation support
    f. Etc.
2. Continue to Step Four: Clarify Roles and Responsibilities

Step Four: Clarify Roles and Responsibilities

Step Four of Workshop Facilitation for Success is Clarify Roles and Responsibilities. Jodi Picoult, author, is quoted as saying, "I woke up one morning thinking about wolves and realized that wolf packs function as families. Everyone has a role, and if you act within the parameters of your role, the whole pack succeeds, and when that falls apart, so does the pack." Understanding roles and responsibilities by the workshop participants is essential to the success and achievement of workshop goals, objectives, and deliverables.

Process to Clarify Roles and Responsibilities:

1. Facilitator and sponsor conduct a kick-off call or meeting with workshop participants to describe:
    a. Workshop purpose and deliverables based on goals and objectives
    b. Participants' roles and responsibilities for before, during, and after the workshop
    c. Preparation and pre-work
2. Facilitator provides participants with pre-work preparation and assignments on the workshop topic
3. Continue to Step Five: Execute the Workshop

Step Five: Execute the Workshop

Step Five of Workshop Facilitation for Success is Execute the Workshop. The charter is set up, the logistics understood, the team is formed, and the roles and responsibilities have been clarified. It is now time to conduct the workshop. Peter Drucker once said, "Plans are only good intentions unless they immediately (result in) hard work." While the facilitator must strive to make the workshop fun, it is truly is hard work for all involved.

Executing the workshop is the step when the facilitator will most often draw on the resources of the Workshop Facilitator's Toolbox section in this handbook in order to apply tools and techniques appropriate and necessary to achieve the goals, objectives, and deliverables defined in the charter. As the following process is executed, refer to the Workshop Facilitator's Toolbox, when necessary and appropriate.

Seven-Step Workshop Facilitation Approach

Process to Execute the Workshop:

1. Sponsor and facilitator kick-off the workshop
   a. Goals, objectives, deliverables, scope, etc.
   b. Introductions, expectations, concerns, ground rules
   c. Participant roles and responsibilities
   d. Agenda items, time, duration
   e. Facilities, snacks, lunches, etc.
2. Participants define and document the current (as is) condition as it relates to the goals and objectives
   a. May develop a SIPOC, RACI, flowchart, input/output map, or deployment flowchart
   b. May conduct a SWOT analysis
3. Participants list issues within the current condition that prevent achievement of the goals and objectives
   a. May conduct brainstorming or nominal group technique; may create affinity diagram or mind map
4. Participants prioritize issues with current condition
   a. May use multi-voting or pairwise comparison
5. Participants determine the cause of the prioritized issues
   a. May use cause-and-effect diagram, cause-and-effect matrix, fault tree analysis, and 5 Why
6. Participants define and document a future-state (ideal) condition, which achieves the goals and objectives
   a. May develop a SIPOC, RACI, flowchart, input/output map, or deployment flowchart
   b. May use solution-selection matrix, decision tree, or Pugh matrix
   c. May create an impact/effort matrix or force field analysis
   d. May conduct FMEA
7. Participants define a workshop action plan to implement the future-state condition, which achieves the goals and objectives
8. Identify owner(s) of the workshop action plan items
9. Identify a workshop action plan implementation team – who, what, and when
   a. Define a close-out plan and timeline; workshop action items should be planned and managed to be completed within 30 days of the workshop and no longer than 90 days
   b. Define a communication plan, training plan, and control plan
10. Continue to Step Six: Share Status of Workshop

Seven-Step Workshop Facilitation Approach

The Workshop Facilitator's Toolbox section of this handbook contains details and instructions on the following summarized tools and techniques:

1. **5 Why Root Cause Analysis** to determine the true root cause of a problem, defect, or issue in terms of why did it occur, why was it not detected, and why was it not prevented
2. **Action Plan** to assign activities to complete tasks post workshop by defining who will complete the activity, what the activity is, when it will be completed, and what is the status
3. **Affinity Diagram** to group ideas or information into common themes or categories in order to conduct further analysis or decision-making activity
4. **Brainstorming** to generate a list of many ideas on a specific topic in an open and free-form thinking environment
5. **Cause-and-Effect (C&E) Diagram** to list and group many potential causes of an effect into categories for further analysis of root cause
6. **Cause-and-Effect Matrix** to compare, rank, and prioritize multiple inputs or causes to many outputs or effects
7. **Communication Plan** to define and manage communication needs based on owner, audience, topic, timing, and delivery method
8. **Conflict Resolution** to manage conflict when it becomes non-productive and disruptive or to mitigate conflict before it occurs
9. **Consensus Building** to gain consensus and support for further actions and efforts
10. **Control Plan** to define and develop a control plan to sustain solutions by managing the process step and characteristics to a specification based on a type of control, sample size, and frequency; to manage corrective action when an out-of-control condition is detected, based on a defined signal
11. **Decision Tree** to define, analyze, and choose between several alternative decisions by understanding the outcomes for each
12. **Fault Tree Analysis (FTA)** to perform actual or potential failure analysis and determine faults or causes of the top-level failure
13. **Force Field Analysis** to determine and manage driving and restraining forces for a goal or idea
14. **Failure Modes and Effects Analysis (FMEA)** to identify and manage the effects, severity, and ability to detect potential failure modes of a solution or process

Seven-Step Workshop Facilitation Approach

15. **Impact/Effort Analysis** to evaluate multiple ideas or solutions against the effort to implement and the benefit from implementing; impact/effort may be replaced with cost/benefit based on the needs of the analysis
16. **Mind Mapping** to use in a brainstorming session to visually represent and analyze ideas in a pictorial-style thinking approach
17. **Multivoting** to reduce or refine a list of many ideas to a shorter, more manageable list; multivoting may be conducted more than once on the same list, if necessary
18. **Nominal Group Technique (NGT)** is a form of combining brainstorming and multivoting to involve all of the participants and avoid conflict in personalities and rank
19. **Pairwise Comparison** to prioritize and rank multiple options, criteria, categories, skills, etc., relative to each other (also known as paired comparison)
20. **Process Maps** to define and document current-state (as is) condition and future-state (ideal) condition and processes using flow diagrams, input/output process maps, and swimlane maps for cross-functional processes
21. **Pugh Matrix** to define, prioritize, and select among many potential concepts by comparing each against the baseline design and weighted design criteria
22. **RACI** to assign roles and responsibilities in the categories of **R**esponsible, **A**ccountable, **C**onsulted, and **I**nformed
23. **SIPOC** to summarize process components in the categories of **S**upplier, **I**nputs, **P**rocess, **O**utputs, and **C**ustomer
24. **Six Thinking Hats** to facilitate a structured thinking process using six metaphorical hats; participants are guided to think in similar ways, such as black hat for understanding risk, blue hat to focus on process, green hat for creativity, red hat to use intuition, white hat for understanding facts, and yellow hat to find value and benefits
25. **Solution-Selection Matrix** to define, prioritize, and select among many potential solutions by comparing each against weighted selection criteria
26. **SWOT Analysis** to analyze current situations in the internal categories of strengths and weaknesses and the external elements of opportunities and threats
27. **Team Building** to manage through team formation phases of forming, storming, norming, and performing and build high-performing teams to achieve results
28. **Training Plan** to define and document a training plan in two

Seven-Step Workshop Facilitation Approach

elements; element one is to analyze, design, and develop; element two is to deliver, evaluate, adjust, and validate

Step Six: Share Status of Workshop

Step Six of Workshop Facilitation for Success is Share Status of Workshop. Key to Workshop Facilitation for Success is timely, concise, and appropriate status updates and communication. Anthony Robbins is credited with the quote, "Skill in the art of communication is crucial to a leader's success; one can accomplish nothing unless one can communicate effectively." As you execute the seven-step workshop facilitation approach, you must ensure that in each step careful consideration is given to the impact on the many and various stakeholders and how that impact is communicated.

Process to Share Status of Workshop:

1. Participants conduct a workshop status report-out at the end of the workshop with the sponsor and key stakeholders
    a. Participants, not the facilitator, present the workshop status report-out
    b. Participants secure approval to proceed with the workshop action plan
2. Workshop action plan owner conducts weekly team update calls on managing the action plan assignments until completion; workshop action items should be managed to be completed within 30 days of the workshop and no longer than 90 days
3. Workshop action plan owner and team conduct sponsor updates based on the communication plan
4. Workshop action plan owner conducts a close-out call with the sponsor when all workshop action items are complete
5. Continue to Step Seven: Salute the Team

Step Seven: Salute the Team

Step Seven of Workshop Facilitation for Success is Salute the Team. Poet Senora Roy once said, "We can accomplish more together than we would dream possible working by ourselves." Recognizing and celebrating the team's success and contributions is key to future workshops' abilities to deliver planned and expected results.

Seven-Step Workshop Facilitation Approach

Process to Salute the Team:

1. Facilitator, action plan owner, and sponsor conduct team recognition and action plan close-out celebration

Benefits of saluting the team include:

- Provide sense of purpose
- Communicate business results
- Reinforce positive outcomes
- Collaborative environment
- Sense of belonging
- Skill development and learning
- Silos and barriers do not exist
- Efficiently and effectively resolve issues that individuals alone cannot resolve
- Inclusive environment in which teams work toward common goals

Methods and approaches to saluting the team include:

- Monthly newsletter
- Website and intranet
- Special celebration and recognition meeting
- Company gifts (logo hats, shirts, mugs, etc.)
- Gift certificates
- Team, staff, and leadership meetings

Saluting the team should be carried out in a public forum, providing team members with recognition and motivation from leadership and peers. This step in Workshop Facilitation for Success ensures that team members will support the next workshop and others will be motivated to join future workshop sessions.

Employing the seven-step process of Workshop Facilitation for Success results in rapid and successful execution of goals, objectives, and deliverables.

Workshop Facilitator's Toolbox

The following chapters make up the Workshop Facilitator's Toolbox and provide facilitators with the tools and techniques necessary to conduct a successful workshop.

5 Why Root Cause Analysis

Have you ever felt that you had solved a problem only to discover it is recurring? Likely the solution was applied to a symptom of the problem, rather than the actual root cause of the problem. Asking "why" five times is a great way to find the true root cause of a problem or defect, and lead to a solution, which will prevent recurrence. Sakichi Toyoda, the founder of Toyota Industries, developed the use of 5 Why in the 1930s as part of an evolving manufacturing process.

The 5 Why root cause analysis technique can be used as a stand-alone problem-solving tool, in combination with cause-and-effect analysis, or as an element of other tools and approaches.

Use 5 Why root cause analysis when:

- Root cause in not known
- Team approach and input are preferred
- Little or no quantitative data is available

Benefits of using 5 Why root cause analysis:

- Facilitate and identify root cause
- Determine root cause before solution
- Provide a collaborative team environment
- Bring together diverse backgrounds and experiences
- Save cost and time by determining and mitigating the root cause

Root-Cause Flow-Down Example
List Problem or Defect

Why Cause Cause
Why Cause Cause Cause Why
Why Cause Cause Cause Why
Why Cause Root Cause Why
     Root Cause
     Cause   Root
             Cause

5 Why Root Cause Process:

1. Ask and write down why the problem or defect occurred, why it was not detected, and why it was not prevented, using the following 5 Why Root Cause Analysis template
2. Continue to ask "why" and write down responses until the root cause(s) is/are determined; the standard number of "why" questions is five, however it may take fewer or more to get to the true root cause; asking "why" may result in more than one answer, requiring branching to more than one root cause, as depicted in the root cause flow-down image

VALUE GENERATION PARTNERS — 5 Why Root-Cause Analysis

Facilitator:			Date:
Problem Statement:			
Why	Why did the Problem or Defect Occur?	Why was it not Detected?	Why was it not Prevented?
1st Why			
2nd Why			
3rd Why			
4th Why			
5th Why			

Action Plan

A well-executed action plan is essential to the success of the post workshop goals, objectives, and deliverables. As quoted by Tom Landry, "Setting a goal is not the main thing. It is deciding how you will go about achieving it and staying with that plan."

An action plan is useful when:

- Post workshop activities are necessary
- Post workshop activities are defined by ownership and due date
- The facilitator, sponsor, and team wish to monitor progress and status of post workshop activities

Workshop Facilitator's Toolbox

Benefits of an action plan include:

- Provide a collaborative team environment
- Save cost and time by managing post workshop activities
- Increase focus and attention on post workshop activities and due dates
- Provide a consistent approach for efficiently and effectively managing post workshop activities

The action plan process defined below is an ideal approach for managing post workshop activities.

Action Plan Process:

1. Define and document post workshop activities necessary to achieve the goals, objectives, and deliverables
2. Determine and assign ownership of the post workshop activities
3. Develop and document due dates for post workshop activities
4. Monitor and report the status of the post workshop activities as part of status updates

This following image depicts a basic action plan template, along with its elements.

	Who	What	Why	When		How	Other
#	Owner	Activity	Reason	Plan Date	Status	Approach	Comments
1					Not Started		
2					Not Started		
3					Not Started		
4					Not Started		
5					Not Started		
6					Not Started		
7					Not Started		

Affinity Diagram

Affinity diagram – also known as KJ Method, for Kawakita Jiro, who developed the technique in the 1960s – is a simple and powerful tool for grouping many ideas and data into natural themes.

Workshop Facilitator's Toolbox

Affinity diagrams may be used to:

- Group and understand existing data, such as
    - Voice of the customer
    - Surveys and interviews
    - Warranty and call logs
- Group and understand new data, such as brainstorming ideas on a specific topic
- Facilitate creative thinking
- Facilitate consensus

Creating an affinity diagram for new data requires facilitation skills and an understanding of brainstorming techniques.

Benefits of creating an affinity diagram include:

- Provide an approach to identify and group similar ideas into logical themes
- Provide a collaborative team environment
- Bring together diverse backgrounds and experiences

Affinity Diagram Process:

1. Silently jot down on a Post-it® note or 3x5 index card – using a verb and a noun – one idea or phrase
2. Randomly post the ideas on a board or wall, with no discussion or evaluation
3. Silently read, sort, and group the ideas into common themes
    a. It may be necessary to limit the number of ideas per theme group
    b. Participants may wish to sort and group themed ideas into sub-themes
4. Define and name the themes based on the content of the ideas
5. Prioritize or vote for most important theme for further work or analysis

Workshop Facilitator's Toolbox

    a. Themes may be used for design or problem-solving efforts
    b. Themes may be used as input to additional tools, such as cause-and-effect diagram

An example of using affinity diagram is typified by a team tasked with the reduction of infection rates in a hospital operating room. The team brainstorms nearly 70 potential ideas intended to reduce infection rates. An affinity diagram is used to group the ideas into six major themes. Then, those six themes are further evaluated and defined for implementation.

Brainstorming

Brainstorming is likely the single most beneficial tool for generating powerful and useful ideas in a group or team environment. It is an efficient and effective method for generating ideas within a team by allowing participants to be creative, unbound by current paradigms. Alex F. Osborn, known as the father of brainstorming, is quoted as saying, "It is easier to tone down a wild idea than to think up a new one."

Brainstorming ground rules:

- No idea is a bad idea
- Encourage participation from all group members
- Do not evaluate, criticize, or judge ideas
- Solicit quantity of ideas
- No titles in the room
- Record ideas; build on those ideas

Brainstorming may be used when:

- There is a desire to generate many ideas
- Team approach and input are preferred
- Little or no quantitative data is available
- Creative thinking and problem solving are useful

Benefits of brainstorming include:

- Provide a collaborative team environment
- Provide a consistent approach for generating ideas

- Bring together diverse backgrounds and experiences
- Provide an approach for fun, creative thinking, and new ideas
- Provide an effective and efficient approach for generating ideas

Brainstorming Process:

1. Allow participants a few minutes in silence to think about ideas related to the brainstorming topic and session deliverables; participants will have been briefed and prepared for the topic prior to conducting the session
2. In a free-flow setting, ask participants to share their ideas with no discussion or evaluation
3. The facilitator records each idea exactly as presented on a flip chart
4. Continue presenting and recording ideas until participants have no additional ideas to add to the list or the agreed-upon time limit is reached
5. Use the brainstorming ideas for the next phase of the workshop, such as action plan, affinity diagram, impact/effort matrix, multi-voting, Pugh matrix, solution-selection matrix, etc.

Cause-and-Effect (C&E) Diagram

A simple yet powerful tool to use in a workshop to quickly generate a list of many potential causes for an effect, problem, or outcome is the cause-and-effect diagram. It's also known as a fishbone diagram for its shape, as well as the Ishikawa diagram for its inventor Kaoru Ishikawa, who developed the technique in the late 1960s.

The cause-and-effect diagram is much like an affinity diagram in that the potential causes are grouped and listed in categories or themes. One major difference is that the groups are identified first, and the brainstorming is intended to come up with ideas to list within each defined group. There are standard categories listed in the following table, which can be used, or the categories can be derived based on the process, problem, or effect, which the diagram represents.

Workshop Facilitator's Toolbox

Manufacturing Industry	Service Industry	Marketing Industry
• Manpower • Mother Nature • Machines • Materials • Methods • Measurements	• Safety • Skills • Systems • Suppliers • Surroundings	• People • Price • Promotion • Place • Product • Process • Physical Evidence

When to use a cause-and-effect diagram:

- There are many varying opinions for the cause
- Team approach and team input are preferred
- Little or no quantitative data is available
- As a precursor to root cause analysis
- As an input to a data collection plan

Benefits of a cause-and-effect diagram include:

- Place cause before solution
- Facilitate root cause analysis
- Provide a collaborative team environment
- Bring together diverse backgrounds and experiences
- Provide an approach to group causes into logical categories
- Save cost and time by determining and mitigating the true root cause

Cause-and-Effect Diagram Process:

1. Facilitate the session by stating and securing consensus for the problem or effect in the form of a "why" question (Example: Why are service calls taking six or more hours per call?)
2. Determine and secure consensus for the cause categories using the standard categories or others specific to the process related to the problem or effect
3. Draw the cause-and-effect diagram, listing the problem or effect and the categories for potential causes
4. Brainstorm potential causes for each of the listed categories
5. Prioritize or vote for most important potential causes for further analysis or use as input to additional tools, such as 5 Why root

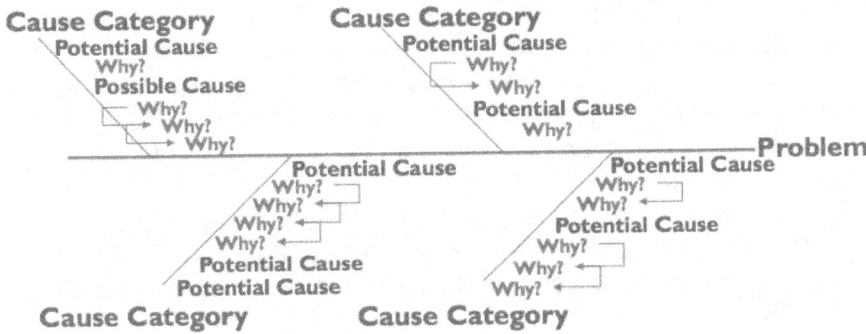

cause analysis

Cause-and-Effect (X-Y) Matrix

A simple yet powerful tool to use in a workshop to determine a relationship between multiple causes and effects is a cause-and-effect matrix. The cause-and-effect matrix is used to determine the most important causes as related to the effects. Also known as an X-Y Matrix, it may be used to describe and understand relationships between process inputs (Xs) and process outputs (Ys).

A cause-and-effect matrix may be useful when:

- Conducting root cause analysis
- Team approach and input are preferred
- Little or no quantitative data is available
- Developing a control plan
- Defining critical process inputs relative to process outputs
- Opinions vary on the relationships between causes and effects

Benefits of a cause-and-effect matrix include:

- Provide a collaborative team environment
- Provide an approach to prioritize causes or inputs
- Save cost and time by determining critical causes or process inputs
- Bring together diverse backgrounds and experiences
- Facilitate root cause analysis, placing cause before solution

Workshop Facilitator's Toolbox

Cause-and-Effect Matrix Process:

1. Draw the cause-and-effect matrix on the board or project an electronic cause-and-effect matrix on a screen
2. List the effects or process outputs across the top of the matrix; these may come from the SIPOC, process maps, critical-to-customer (CTC) characteristics, critical-to-quality (CTQ), or brainstorming
3. Determine the weight or importance of the effects or process outputs, and enter into the "weight" row of the matrix; weights may be determined using pairwise comparison or simply ranking on a scale of 1 to 5
4. List the causes or process inputs along the left side of the matrix; these may come from the SIPOC, process maps, cause-and-effect diagram, or brainstorming
5. Enter a relationship value of 1 for weak, 5 for medium, or 9 for strong, in the association table for each entry
6. Use the highest rank score and highest percent rank score to determine where to focus the team's activities for the next phase of the workshop; note that rank and percent rank scores are calculated by a formula in the matrix

Example: A manufacturer of LED flat screen televisions is working to reduce five recurring defects found during the final inspection and test process. The quality improvement team lists the five defect types as effects across the top of the matrix and the process inputs as the causes on the side of the matrix. The team gives each process input a score of 1, 5, or 9, relative to each of the defects or effects. The team then uses score results to determine process inputs that have the strongest relationships to the defects and on which to focus improvement efforts in order to reduce the defects.

This following image depicts a basic cause-and-effect matrix template, along with its elements.

Workshop Facilitator's Toolbox

VALUE GENERATION PARTNERS — Cause-and-Effect Matrix

Workshop Name:
Workshop Facilitator:
Date:

		1	2	3	4	5	6	7	8	9	10		Rank	% Rank
	Effects (Y's) Outputs													
	Weight (1 to 5)													
Causes (X's) Inputs		Association Table (1 = weak, 5 = medium, or 9 = strong)											Rank	% Rank
1														
2														
3														
4														
5														
6														
7														
8														
9														
10														

Communication Plan

A well-executed communication plan is essential to the success of a workshop. Anthony Robbins is quoted as saying, "To effectively communicate, we must realize that we are all different in the way we perceive the world and use this understanding as a guide to our communication with others." And George Bernard Shaw was quoted as saying, "The single biggest problem in communication is the illusion that it has taken place." Both quotes signify the importance of a well-developed and well-executed communication plan.

Benefits of a workshop communication plan include:

- Facilitates securing support for your workshop
- Socialization and clarification of the workshop charter
- Clarification of roles and responsibilities

Workshop Facilitator's Toolbox

- Shares status of the workshop action plan and training plan
- Updates on workshop issues, risks, and changes

Communication Plan development and maintenance process:

1. Workshop facilitator, with input from sponsor and team, makes communication topic entries on the communication plan template
2. Communication topic owners conduct communications, as described on the communication plan
3. Action plan/communication plan owner reviews the communication plan with team during workshop status review meetings
4. New communication topic entries or adjustments are entered in the plan and reviewed during workshop status review meetings

The following image depicts a basic communication plan template, along with its elements.

VALUE GENERATION PARTNERS	Communication Management Plan					
Workshop Name:			Workshop Facilitator:			
Who		What	When	Why	Where/How	Other
Owner	Audience	Topic	Timing	Intent	Delivery Channel	Comments

Informative Communication

Rather far, relatively short, very small, extremely heavy, fairly new, too many, very long, pretty old, oversized, a lot, completely undersized, too few, quite large, very late. In everyday conversation, these words are perfectly fine, yet in defining workshop goals and objectives, these words are not truly informative.

So, why do I suggest these words are not informative, when they're used all the time? Have you ever attended a workshop report-out meeting that went something like this? "The process takes way too long, so we are going to shorten it a lot." You would most certainly say that was not informative. Obviously I'm kidding; no experienced

Workshop Facilitator's Toolbox

workshop facilitator would use these words to describe a process or an initiative, however it is important to instill a culture of clear communication and informative reporting.

Let's explore an example of using non-informational words in everyday life:

- There are <u>a lot</u> of people ahead of us in line at the movie ticket counter.

What is meant by "a lot" of people? Is it five, 10, or more? A lot can mean different things to different people, or even different things to the same person based on varying circumstances. If I arrive at the ticket counter just as the movie is about to begin, then a lot of people might very well be five; yet if I arrive at the ticket counter 15 minutes before the movie is about to start, a lot may be a dozen. A lot to you might be 15; for me, under the same circumstances, a lot might be six.

Let's explore some other examples:

- I can't make it to the store and back home in time for the movie, because it's <u>extremely far</u>.
    - How far is the store from the house – two miles, 10 miles, more than 25 miles?
- My car is considered a classic because it's <u>very old</u>.
    - How old is the car – five years, 15 years, 50 years?
- I can't lift these boxes, because they're <u>awfully heavy</u>.
    - How heavy are the boxes – five pounds, 50 pounds, more than 100 pounds?
- Please don't leave without me; I'll be there <u>soon</u>.
    - How soon will you be – an hour, 30 minutes, 15 minutes or less?

What if the sentences were written like this?

- I can't make it to the store and back home in time for the movie, because it's <u>10 miles one way</u>.
- My car is considered a classic, because it's <u>35 years old</u>.
- I can't lift these boxes, because they're <u>more than 100 pounds each</u>.

Workshop Facilitator's Toolbox

- Please don't leave without me; I'll be there in <u>20 minutes</u>.

Do the rewritten sentences provide more factual and useful information? Great! So let's get back to the workshop and informative reporting. When defining workshop goals, writing a workshop charter, writing a workshop summary, or reporting out the status of an improvement initiative, take the time to be informative and factual with your words. You will generate a greater understanding of and stronger support for your efforts.

Concise Communications

In the interest of this chapter's topic, I'll keep it concise – meaning it will be brief, yet comprehensive. Concise reporting, presentations, and writing are as important in transformation and operational excellence workshops, as in any other field of practice. Concise communication carries forward in the documentation of a workshop description or goal, a workshop status report, and a workshop presentation for a group of stakeholders.

I imagine you can remember a presentation you attended or a report you received that went on, and on, and on, and on? These types of run-on communications tend to leave us more confused than informed. It is possible to be brief and to convey important information, as seen in the important works of the Pythagorean Theorem, referenced in 24 words, and Archimedes' Principle, referenced in 67 words. Even Chinese proverbs are famous for being short, and chock-full of wisdom.

As you coach and mentor your workshop team in continuous improvement methodologies, you may also include discussion and training around concise reporting. Train them to determine the objective of the communication, to know their audience, and to plan accordingly. Workshop facilitators should understand that the first few minutes or words of a communication are critical; they need to convey the important message and hook the audience. Workshop facilitators should spend time reviewing, practicing, and refining their reports and presentations to find the perfect balance between detail and brevity, thereby meeting the intent of concise reporting.

Conflict Resolution

Conflict is natural and inevitable. Workshop teams are comprised of individuals from diverse backgrounds, with varying experiences, skills, goals, and opinions. Conflict results from differences in motivations and opinions, expressed by emotional responses, such as frustration, fear, anger, and excitement. Wellness author and speaker Greg Anderson is quoted as saying, "The Law of Win/Win says, 'Let's not do it your way or my way; let's do it the best way'."

Benefits of healthy conflict resolution include:

- Provide a collaborative team environment
- Provide an environment where silos and barriers do not exist
- Increase focus and attention on a sustainable workshop results
- Establish workshop ground rules where the expectation is to respectfully, constructively resolve issues
- Provide an inclusive environment in which individuals with diverse experience, skills, and backgrounds work together on common goals

It is helpful to recognize symptoms of conflict, and more importantly, to determine and eliminate – or prevent – actual causes of conflict.

Symptoms of conflict include:

- Impatience with other team members
- Mistrust and lack of understanding
- Arguing; defending positions and ideas
- Ideas and suggestions are unconnected; not building on others' ideas and suggestions
- Distortion of facts and information to support personal agendas

Causes of conflict include:

- Threats to status and organizational structure
- Pressures from roles, responsibilities
- Differences in perceptions, values
- Differences in standards
- Clashes in motivations, behaviors
- Inconsistencies in priorities, goals

Workshop Facilitator's Toolbox

- Changes in processes, procedures

Considerations for preventing conflict:

- Appreciate limitations of arguing and debating
- Believe that ideas and solutions can be mutually acceptable
- Understand that conflict is a natural, healthy element of decision making
- Acknowledge that differences in ideas are useful and lead to creative solutions
- Openness to others' ideas and suggestions, with a willingness to examine possibilities
- Recognizing that some of the best ideas and solutions are generated through conflict resolution

Conflict Resolution Process:

1. Identify conflict source and root cause
2. Define potential solutions to cause of conflict
3. Develop and act on a mutual agreement on an acceptable solution to the conflict

Considerations for resolving conflict:

- Encourage participants to propose and select the best solution
- Determine how important the issue is to all participants
- Listen carefully to each person's point of view; separate areas of agreement from disagreement
- Ask participants how the process may be improved; evaluate costs versus gains
- Ensure all parties understand their responsibilities, including dealing with the problem and the solution

Tools and techniques useful for conflict resolution include:

- Cause-and-effect matrix
- Decision tree
- Fault tree analysis
- Force field analysis
- Impact/effort matrix
- Pairwise comparison

Workshop Facilitator's Toolbox

- Six thinking hats
- Solution-selection matrix

Consensus Building

Building consensus is an essential behavior to integrate into the workshop process and approach; it is a key element ensuring ideas are supported and actions are executed with ownership and accountability. Consensus building is the resolution of conflict and disagreement in order to reach a collaborative agreement with solidarity and harmony. It is a group decision and collective agreement, which is supported and carried forward by the group. Martin Luther King, Jr. is quoted as saying, "A genuine leader is not a searcher for consensus, but a molder of consensus."

Merriam-Webster defines consensus as:

- A general agreement about something
- An idea or opinion that is shared by all people in a group
- A judgment arrived at by most of those concerned

Synonyms of consensus include accord, agreement, concurrence, harmony, and solidarity. Antonyms of consensus are conflict, disagreement, disunity, and discord.

Benefits of consensus building include:

- Provide a collaborative team environment
- Provide a consistent approach for making decisions
- Provide support and ownership of decisions
- Increase focus and attention on decision making

Consensus Building Process:

1. Define the topic, issue, problem of the workshop
2. Define session process and ground rules
3. Identify alternatives, such as solutions and options, to the workshop topic
4. Conduct decision-making process to formulate agreement and consensus
5. Carry the decision forward to the next step or phase

Workshop Facilitator's Toolbox

Elements of consensus building:

- It is not a win or lose situation
- Avoid debating and arguing over ideas
- Use ground rules established by the team
- State position with facts and respect
- Use proven facilitation tools and techniques
- Differences of opinion are natural and healthy; ensure they are stated in a respectful manner
- Involve the entire team in the decision-making process
- Ensure every member will support the decision
- No one leaves the session in silent disagreement

Tools and techniques useful for consensus building:

- Affinity diagram
- Brainstorming
- Cause-and-effect matrix
- Decision tree
- Fault tree analysis
- Force field analysis
- Impact/effort matrix
- Multivoting
- Nominal group technique
- Pairwise comparison
- Pugh matrix
- Six thinking hats
- Solution-selection matrix

It can be beneficial to include a thumbs up/down/sideways technique when facilitating consensus building with a workshop team. It allows all of the members to participate in the decision in a visual manner, and it may lighten the mood and discussions during the process.

The "thumbs" approach goes as follows:

- Thumbs up – in complete agreement with the decision
- Thumbs down – in complete disagreement with the decision
- Thumbs sideways – not in total agreement, but will support the decision

Control Plan

A control plan is essentially a summary of the types of process controls that will be used to monitor and control critical process characteristics. It is a method for assuring that improvements will be sustained once process changes have been implemented. Process controls can also be used for any process to ensure that the process continues to perform at the desired level. A control plan should be reviewed periodically to ensure it is current and effective.

A control plan is used when:

- The workshop results in changes to the process, product, or service
- The workshop results in changes in roles and responsibilities
- A product or service includes critical characteristics
- Products or services move across changes in ownership
- Prior to a product or service reaching an irreversible point in the process

Common types of process controls include:

- Layered audits
- Process audits
- Internal audits
- Help chains
- Automated controls
- In-process inspections
- Statistical Process Control (SPC)
- Total Preventive Maintenance (TPM)

Workshop Facilitator's Toolbox

Benefits of a control plan include:

- Increase focus and attention on process control points
- Provide a consistent approach for identifying and controlling critical process input characteristics
- Provide an approach to ensure conformance to specifications and customer requirements
- Save cost and time by identifying and controlling critical process input characteristics

Considerations when creating a control plan include:

- What input variables are critical to process performance?
- What process characteristics will be monitored?
- At what point in the process is it best to monitor key input characteristics?
- What are the specifications of the characteristics to be monitored?
- What type of control method will be used?
- How often is the characteristic measured and what is the sample size?
- How will the characteristic be measured?
- Who will be responsible for monitoring the characteristic and taking the measurements?
- What is the signal to indicate an out-of-control condition?
- What is the corrective action for an out-of-control condition?
- Who is responsible for the corrective action?

Control Plan Development Process:

1. Review process steps and control plan inputs such as:
    a. Warranty issues
    b. Quality issues
    c. Customer complaints
    d. Process maps and diagrams
    e. Failure Modes and Effects Analysis (FMEA)
    f. Cause-and-Effect Diagram
    g. Cause-and-Effect Matrix/X-Y Matrix
2. Determine the control characteristics, control points, and type of control
3. Determine the frequency, sample size, responsibility, and

measurement method
4. Determine the out-of-control signal, owner, and corrective action
5. Implement the control plan

The following image depicts a basic control plan template, along with its elements.

Workshop Name:				Workshop Facilitator:				Date:		
What				When	Who	How	What	Who	How	Other
Operation & Process Step	Characteristic	Specification & Tolerance	Type of Control	Frequency & Sample Size	Responsible	Measurement Method	Signal	Responsible	Corrective Action	Comments

Decision Tree

A decision tree is a useful tool for defining, analyzing, and choosing between several alternative decisions by understanding the outcomes for each. It is a tree diagram visually displaying alternative decisions, including probability, expected value, and outcome for each. It may be used in combination with other decision-making tools, such as Pugh matrix or solution-selection matrix.

A decision tree may be useful when:

- Little quantitative data is available
- It is necessary to make a decision from among several alternatives
- Opinions vary on the best decision
- The decision will result in considerable expense and potential risks

Benefits of a decision tree include:

- Fun; easy to use and understand
- Can be conducted alone or with a team; if facilitated with a team, it will bring together diverse backgrounds and experiences and it will provide a collaborative team environment
- Support decision making when little data is available

Workshop Facilitator's Toolbox

- Provide input to additional decision-making approaches
- Ability to build in new scenarios and outcomes
- Provide an approach to analyze, challenge, and prioritize alternative decisions
- Provide an approach to determine probability, expected values, and consequences of alternative decisions

Common decision tree symbols include:

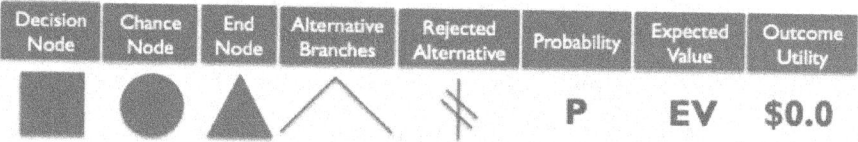

Below is an example of a decision tree diagram with "Software Solution" as the subject of the decision.

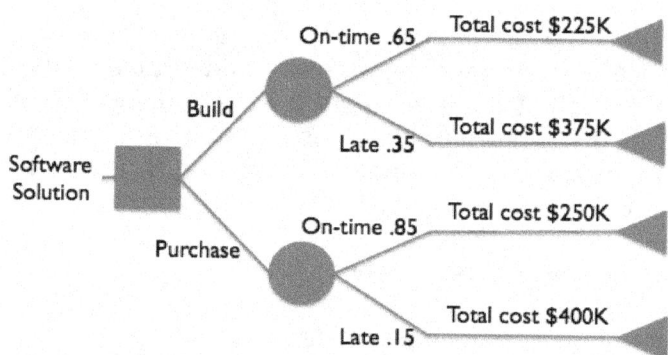

Decision Tree Process:

1. Define the subject for which you must make a decision; inputs to a decision tree may include goal setting, solution selection, determining a course of action, creating a strategic direction, solving a problem, etc.
2. Document the subject of the decision tree on paper or flip chart, or in an electronic format
3. Add potential decisions to the decision tree subject
4. Add probability and outcome for each decision
5. Validate that all decision choices, probabilities, and outcomes have been considered and are added to the decision tree

6. Analyze the decision tree to determine the best decision choice using probabilities, outcomes, and expected values to support the final decision

Fault Tree Analysis (FTA)

Fault tree analysis is an effective tool for actual or potential failure analysis, followed by correction or prevention techniques. Originally developed in the early 1960s, fault tree analysis (FTA) was used to conduct top-down failure analysis. Primarily used in safety and reliability engineering for preventive analysis to reduce risk and prevent failure, FTA is now used in a wide range of industries and scenarios.

Fault tree analysis may be conducted to determine root cause of failure as a reactive tool, or to predict preventive analysis of potential failures as a proactive tool. In either scenario, FTA starts with a single top-level event or failure, which is analyzed to determine actual or potential input faults and their root causes. An action plan to eliminate or prevent causes of input faults to the top-level failure is determined and launched as a result of the fault tree analysis.

The following image depicts a basic fault tree diagram example.

Fault tree top-level, input/fault, and gate example

Workshop Facilitator's Toolbox

A fault tree analysis may be useful when:

- Quantitative data may be limited
- Opinions vary on the relationships between inputs and the top-level failure
- It is desirable to understand and correct – or prevent – causes of the top-level failure
- It is necessary and important to prioritize inputs that could lead to the top-level failure
- Failure prevention efforts take place for a system or product in the design phase

Benefits of a fault tree analysis include:

- May be conducted alone or with a team; if facilitated with a team, it will bring together diverse backgrounds and experiences and it will provide a collaborative team environment
- Facilitate reactive or preventive root cause analysis
- Provide an approach to analyze and prioritize inputs or faults
- Identify and eliminate – or prevent – causes of the top-level failure
- Improve safety, reliability, and performance of systems and products
- Design systems and products to prevent potential causes of the top-level failure

Common fault tree symbols include:

- Basic Event – Failure event in a process, system, or component requiring no additional analysis
- External Event – An event that is normally expected to occur
- Undeveloped Event – An event where information is not available or is determined to be unimportant
- Conditioning Event – A condition or restriction applied to a logic gate
- Intermediate Event – Used to include additional event information
- Transfer In/Out – Used to indicate a transfer to a related fault tree
- Or Gate – The event occurs if one or more of the input events occur
- And Gate – The event occurs if all of the input events occur

- Exclusive Or Gate – The event occurs if one and only one input event occurs
- Priority And Gate – The event occurs if all of the input events occur in a specific order
- Inhibit Gate – The event occurs if the input event occurs, along with a conditional input event

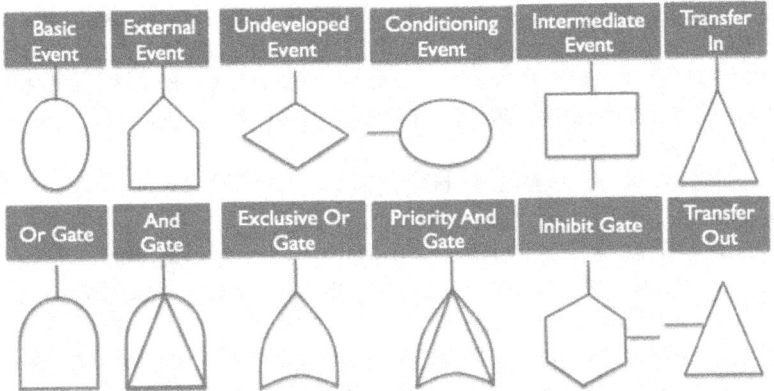

Fault Tree Analysis Process:

1. Select and clearly define the top-level failure for analysis with fault tree (one top-level failure per fault tree); inputs to a fault tree analysis may include defect records, warranty records, service logs, customer complaint logs, system performance requirements, FMEA, etc.
2. Under the top-level failure, add inputs or faults, which may or do contribute to the top-level failure
3. Under each input or fault, list all actual or potential causes of failure; if available, list the probabilities for each cause
4. Draw the fault tree diagram (top-level failure – logic gates – inputs or faults – logic gates – actual or potential causes) using the basic fault tree symbols and logic gates
5. Analyze the fault tree to determine actual or potential root cause(s) of the top-level failure; using a cause-and-effect diagram and/or 5 Why root cause analysis at this step may be useful to determine root cause(s)
6. Define and launch an action plan (who, what, when) to correct existing root cause(s)

An example of using fault tree analysis is when an engineering team is formed to determine and prevent potential causes of car door airbags not deploying on a side impact. The team lists "car door airbags not deploying on side impact" as the top-level failure on a fault tree. They use design specifications, historical data, and crash test results to determine actual and potential input faults to the top-level failure, along with their associated causes. The information is used to create a fault tree, analyze it for root cause of the input faults, and conduct tests to validate assumptions. The team creates an action plan to implement corrections to the design to prevent actual and potential causes of the faults and top-level failure.

Force Field Analysis

Kurt Lewin's 1940s Force Field Analysis is a very powerful, yet simple, tool to evaluate opposing forces (drivers and restrainers) and to determine actions for moving toward achieving a goal or objective. Force field analysis' use has expanded over the years from its origins in social science to being used in a variety of business situations. It is a proactive approach to understand variables and forces around a particular goal or objective, and to act on the variables in a positive manner.

Force field analysis may be used when:

- A workshop decision or solution idea is being evaluated for feasibility
- A new process, product, or service is being evaluated for viability
- There is concern for sustainability of ideas and solutions
- A new solution is being evaluated for implementation

Benefits of force field analysis include:

- Proactive approach to define and mitigate restraining forces
- Provide input for developing an action plan and assigning activities
- Provide input for a communication plan
- Provide input for directional changes for workshop ideas and solutions
- Provide a collaborative team environment
- Bring together diverse backgrounds and experiences

Workshop Facilitator's Toolbox

Follow the steps below for a simple approach to conducting a force field analysis session:

1. Construct a force field analysis diagram on a flipchart or use a template projected onto the screen
2. Validate the current situation or problem
3. List the goal or objective of the analysis
4. List the driving forces, and rank forces from 1 to 5, with 5 being the strongest
5. List the restraining forces, and rank the forces from 1 to 5, with 5 being the strongest
6. Define an action plan describing "who, what, and when" to leverage or strengthen drivers, and to mitigate or eliminate restrainers
7. Execute and manage the action plan to ensure success

An example of using force field analysis is a cross-functional team tasked with implementing a new resource planning software solution. The team uses a force field analysis to understand the drivers, which would be leveraged or strengthened, and the restrainers, which must be eliminated or mitigated, to be successful with the new implementation. The information from the force field analysis helps the team define the action plan.

The following image depicts a basic force field analysis template, along with its elements.

VALUE GENERATION PARTNERS	Force Field Analysis		
Facilitator:		Date:	
Goal/Objective			
List Drivers	Score	List Restrainers	Score
Total Driver Score	0	Total Restrainer Score	0

Workshop Facilitator's Toolbox

Failure Modes and Effects Analysis (FMEA)

While the saying, "If anything can go wrong, it will," has been quoted as Murphy's Law, certainly an addendum to it could be "... and new solutions create new problems." For a new or existing product, process, or service, FMEA is an excellent approach to employ for finding and mitigating potential causes of failures. FMEA was first introduced in the late 1940s by the US Military, adopted and modified in the early 1960s by NASA, and is now widely used in most every industry.

FMEA can be used for:

- Evaluating failures or potential failures for existing services, products, or processes
- Control points for new or existing services, products, or processes
- Improvement opportunities for existing services, products, or processes
- Root cause analysis for existing services, products, or processes

FMEA should be used when:

- The workshop results in a new process, product, or service
- The workshop impacts safety, quality, or customer service
- New solutions will be evaluated and implemented
- Root cause analysis will be performed

Benefits of conducting FMEA include:

- Increase focus and attention on potential failure causes
- Proactive approach for preventing the causes of potential failures from becoming failures
- Provide a consistent approach for analyzing, prioritizing, communicating, and managing potential failures
- Provide an approach to efficiently and effectively mitigate potential failures
- Provide a collaborative team environment
- Save cost and time by identifying, prioritizing, and managing potential failures

Workshop Facilitator's Toolbox

Follow these listed steps for a condensed and simplified version of conducting FMEA.

1. Fill in the FMEA header

VALUE	Failure Modes and Effects Analysis (FMEA)		
Item/Process:	Preparer:	Number:	
Team		Date:	

2. Fill in the process steps or requirements for the FMEA topic

#	Process Function (Step) (Requirements)	Potential Failure Modes (What could go wrong with process inputs, components, information, etc.)	Potential Failure Effects (The effect the failure mode has on the Output or Y variable)	S E V	Potential Causes of the Failure Mode	O C C	Current Process Controls (that could prevent or detect the Cause)	D E T	R P N
1									
2									
3									
4									
5									
6									
7									

3. List potential failure modes for each step in the process or each requirement (There may be multiple failure modes for each)
4. List potential failure effects for each failure mode
5. Rank the "severity" of each potential failure mode and effect (The ranking is typically a 1-to-10 ranking, with 10 being the most severe)

Rating	Description
10	Dangerously high
9	Extremely high
8	Very high
7	High
6	Moderate
5	Low
4	Very Low
3	Minor
2	Very Minor
1	None

6. List potential causes for each potential failure mode
7. Rank the likelihood of "occurrence" for each potential failure mode cause (1-to-10 ranking, 10 is the most likely to occur)

Workshop Facilitator's Toolbox

Rating	Description
10	Very High: Failure is almost inevitable
9	High: Failures occur almost as often as not
8	High: Repeated failures
7	High: Failures occur often
6	Moderately High: Frequent failures
5	Moderate: Occasional failures
4	Moderately Low: Infrequent failures
3	Low: Relatively few failures
2	Low: Failures are few and far between
1	Remote: Failure is unlikely

8. List current process controls for each of the potential failure mode causes
9. Rank current process controls for the "detection" ability of the potential cause or the failure mode after occurrence (1-to-10 ranking, 10 is the most uncertain to detect)

Rating	Description
10	Absolute Uncertainty
9	Very Remote
8	Remote
7	Very Low
6	Low
5	Moderate
4	Moderately High
3	High
2	Very High
1	Almost Certain

10. Calculate the risk priority number (RPN) by multiplying *severity x occurrence x detection* to prioritize actions; the highest (or predetermined cut-off level) RPNs are addressed, along with any company, industry, or customer requirements with high-severity ratings
11. List recommended actions for identified RPNs and high-severity ratings
12. List the responsible person and target dates for each recommended action
13. List action taken and re-rank severity, occurrence, and detection
14. Recalculate the RPN, based on actions taken
15. Repeat the FMEA process, as necessary and as part of continuous improvement cycles

Workshop Facilitator's Toolbox

Recommend Actions	Responsible Person & Target Date	Actions Taken	S E V	O C C	D E T	R P N

Impact/Effort Analysis

An impact/effort analysis is a powerful and simple tool for prioritizing and choosing from many potential options. It is the process of using a matrix-style tool to evaluate several options against the impact gained and effort required for each option or idea.

Impact/effort analysis may be useful when:

- It is necessary to determine which ideas, solutions, etc., to focus on when resources are limited
- Quantitative, objective data is not available as part of the evaluation, selection, and decision-making process
- A choice must be made from several options, and it is necessary to screen the options relative to impact gained and effort required

Benefits of impact/effort analysis include:

- Provide a consistent and efficient approach for prioritizing and choosing from many options
- Reduce emotion and bias from the decision-making and prioritization process
- Provide a collaborative team environment
- Results of many options are displayed on one matrix-style tool

Impact/Effort Analysis Process:

1. Brainstorm a list of potential options for evaluation based on the impact/effort topic or use a prepared list from a previous brainstorming session
2. Construct an impact/effort matrix on a flipchart or use a template projected onto the screen

Workshop Facilitator's Toolbox

3. Evaluate each option for impact gained and effort required, and place the option number or identification in the appropriate impact/effort cell on the matrix
4. Select and focus on the options with the highest impact at the lowest possible effort

The following image depicts a basic impact/effort template, along with its elements.

VALUE GENERATION PARTNERS Impact/Effort Matrix

Project Name:			
Project Manager:			Date:

Impact High			
Impact Medium			
Impact Low			
	Low	Medium	High
	Effort		

An example of using an impact/effort matrix is by an improvement team working together to determine which of many options are best suited to reduce emergency room wait times. The team evaluates each option for impact (how much it would reduce the emergency room wait time) and effort (how difficult and costly it will be to implement). The options with the highest impact and lowest effort are chosen to implement.

While the matrix tool is described using impact and effort as evaluation categories, the same matrix – and approach – may be used to evaluate options against other categories, such as cost/benefit, impact/risk, value/effort, etc. The matrix indicates that the options are evaluated from a low, medium, and high perspective, yet the criteria may be replaced with elements based on specific and organizational needs. For example: Low, medium, and high may be replaced with appropriate dollar values, if the matrix would be used to do a cost/benefit analysis, rather than an impact/effort. As you can see, the matrix categories and criteria may be tailored to your organizational needs.

Mind Mapping

Mind mapping is a powerful, simple tool to use in a brainstorming session to visually represent and analyze ideas. It is a pictorial-style thinking approach, which focuses on one central topic and allows information to be structurally portrayed for analysis and prioritization.

Unlike lists of ideas generated from typical brainstorming approaches, ideas generated through mind mapping connect to a single central topic in a branch-like diagram. Each new idea may generate an additional branch connected directly to the central topic, or expanded as a sub-idea from an existing main idea.

Mind mapping may be useful when:

- Little or no quantitative data is available
- Creative thinking and problem solving are useful
- A team approach and input are preferred
- Organizing and presenting information in a visual method are desired

Benefits of mind mapping include:

- Bring together diverse backgrounds and experiences
- Provide an approach for generating creative thoughts and ideas
- Provide an approach for pictorial presentation of ideas
- Provide a collaborative team environment

Mind Mapping Process:

1. Write the central topic on a board or flip chart
2. Brainstorm, write, and connect main ideas related to the central topic on the board
3. Brainstorm, write, and connect sub-ideas related to the main ideas on the board
4. Continue to brainstorm ideas until no additions are necessary

Workshop Facilitator's Toolbox

5. Use mind map for next phase of the initiative, such as an action plan or prioritization process

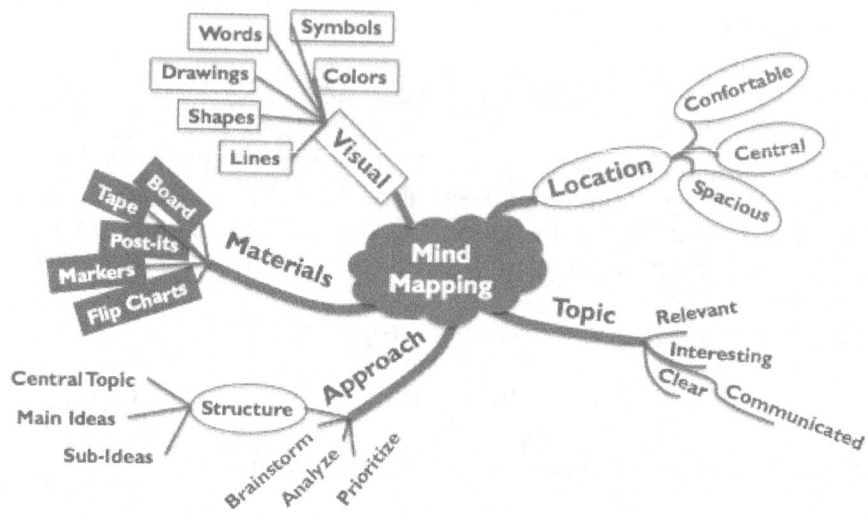

Mind mapping examples:

Central Topic Examples	Potential Main Ideas to Connect to the Central Topic
Plan a Vacation	Destinations, Timing, Length of Stay, Method of Transportation
Plan a Meeting	Location, Duration, Attendees, Agenda
Landscape Yard	Size, Location, Flowers, Shrubbery
Design a Smart Phone	Size, Features, Functionality, Colors, Materials, Manufacturer
Open a Restaurant	Location, Menu, Service Type, Seating Style

The central topics listed in the examples above will be written at the center of the mind map, and the main ideas listed become branches. Participants continue to brainstorm potential main ideas to connect to the central topic and sub-ideas to connect to the main ideas. Once the mind map is complete, participants will evaluate the ideas for relevancy, priority, and next steps.

Workshop Facilitator's Toolbox

Multivoting

Multivoting is a simple, efficient approach for selecting and reaching group consensus on the most important ideas from a list on which to focus. It can be thought of as reducing the trivial many to the critical few.

Multivoting may be used when:

- There are too many ideas on which to focus
- Consensus for selecting ideas is preferred
- Team approach and input are preferred
- Opinions vary on which ideas should take priority

Benefits of multivoting include:

- Provide a collaborative team environment
- Provide a consistent approach for selecting ideas
- Provide an effective and efficient approach for selecting ideas
- Facilitate building consensus
- Save time and cost by focusing on select ideas

Multivoting Process:

1. Write each idea on a flip chart and assign consecutive numbers, starting with one (1) through the entire list of ideas
2. Provide each participant with a limited number of colored dot stickers (usually one-third of the total number of ideas listed)
3. Ask participants to vote on their choice for the top ideas by placing a dot next to an idea
    a. Determine the maximum number of votes each participant may post on a single idea
    b. If appropriate, voting may be done in confidence by asking participants to write on a piece of paper their votes for top choices
4. Record the total number of votes for each idea
    a. If necessary, repeat the multivoting process on the ideas with the highest votes until the list of ideas with the most votes is manageable for taking action
5. Develop an action plan (who, what, and when) for ideas with the most votes

Workshop Facilitator's Toolbox

An example of using multivoting is characterized by a team challenged with determining select ideas, from a list of 20, on which to focus their efforts. A list of brainstorming ideas is developed by the team to reduce customer wait time at a service desk for issuing license plates and car titles in a government office. The team decides to use multivoting to select the top five ideas from the list. Using a cut-off value of five votes after the first round of voting, there are eight ideas remaining on the list. With limited resources and time, the team wishes to reduce the list to five ideas. The team conducts a second round of multivoting on the remaining list of eight ideas; it becomes clear by the number of votes those top five ideas the team feels is most important to implement. There is full support and ownership by the team and sponsor to proceed with implementation of the ideas numbered 2, 5, 6, 10, and 17. See the voting table image for the votes cast in two rounds.

Idea No.	1st Vote Score	New List	2nd Vote Score	Final List
1	0			
2	10	2	7	2
3	0			
4	7	4	0	
5	9	5	6	5
6	6	6	5	6
7	0			
8	6	8	0	
9	0			
10	7	10	6	10
11	0			
12	4			
13	5	13	2	
14	0			
15	3			
16	0			
17	8	17	6	17
18	0			
19	3			
20	2			

Nominal Group Technique (NGT)

Nominal group technique (NGT) is an effective approach to generate, clarify, and prioritize ideas. It is a combination of brainstorming and multivoting, with a twist on the idea-generation component of the process. It provides an approach to include all participants in the discussion process, thus avoiding concerns, conflict, and criticism.

Nominal group technique ground rules:

- No idea is a bad idea

Workshop Facilitator's Toolbox

- Encourage participation from all
- Do not criticize or evaluate ideas
- Solicit quantity of ideas
- No titles in the room
- Record ideas; build on those ideas

Nominal group technique may be used when:

- Strength of personalities vary within the group of participants
- Levels of authority vary within the group of participants
- There is reluctance to participate by some participants
- There are new members to the group
- Topic of the session may be perceived as controversial in nature
- Generating a quantity of ideas is difficult

Benefits of nominal group technique include:

- Provide an approach for equal participation
- Provide a safe, fair environment for participants
- Bring together diverse backgrounds and experiences
- Provide an effective and efficient approach for generating, clarifying, and prioritizing ideas

Nominal Group Technique Process:

1. Allow participants five to ten minutes in silence to generate ideas related to the session topic and deliverables; participants will have been briefed on and prepared for the topic prior to the session
2. In a round robin arrangement, ask each participant to verbally state one idea at a time with no discussion or evaluation; facilitator records each idea on a flip chart exactly as presented; continue presenting and recording ideas until participants have no more ideas to add to the list or the agreed-upon time limit is reached
3. Review and clarify each idea on the list, seeking approval by idea contributor; reword, where necessary; with agreement by participants, strike an idea from the list
4. Prioritize the ideas using impact/effort matrix, multivoting, pairwise comparison, selection matrix, etc.
5. Use these prioritized ideas for the next phase of the initiative,

such as an action plan

Pairwise Comparison

Pairwise comparison (also known as paired comparison) is a powerful and simple tool for prioritizing and ranking multiple options relative to each other. It is the process of using a matrix-style tool to compare each option in pairs and determine which is the preferred choice or has the highest level of importance based on defined criteria. At the end of the comparison process, each option has a rank or relative rating as compared to the rest of the options.

Pairwise comparison may be useful when:

- Quantitative, objective data is not available as part of the evaluation and decision-making process
- It is necessary to determine which programs, projects, problems, etc., to focus on when resources are limited
- A choice must be made from several options, and it is necessary to screen the options relative to each other
- Decision or selection criteria must be weighted or ranked for importance relative to each other prior to using in a decision or selection matrix

Benefits of pairwise comparison include:

- Provide a consistent and efficient approach for prioritizing or ranking multiple options
- Provide a collaborative team environment
- Reduce emotion and bias from the decision-making process

Pairwise Comparison Process:

1. List the options for comparison along the "X" and "Y" axes of the Pairwise Comparison Matrix; in the image, notice that each option is assigned a letter to represent the option in the comparison matrix
2. Determine the criteria for comparison, such as which option is preferred in terms of cost, customer impact, financial impact, resource requirements, risk level, etc.
3. Compare each option in the rows to each option in the columns,

Workshop Facilitator's Toolbox

and place the letter of the preferred or most important option in the cell, which aligns the two options; notice that the matrix does not allow options to be compared to themselves, or to each other more than one time

4. Once all options are compared, sum the number of times each letter appears in the matrix for the prioritization ranking of each option; note that the matrix template performs the calculation; if necessary or useful, convert the rankings to percentages
5. Use the prioritization ranking of the options for the next phase of the decision-making process

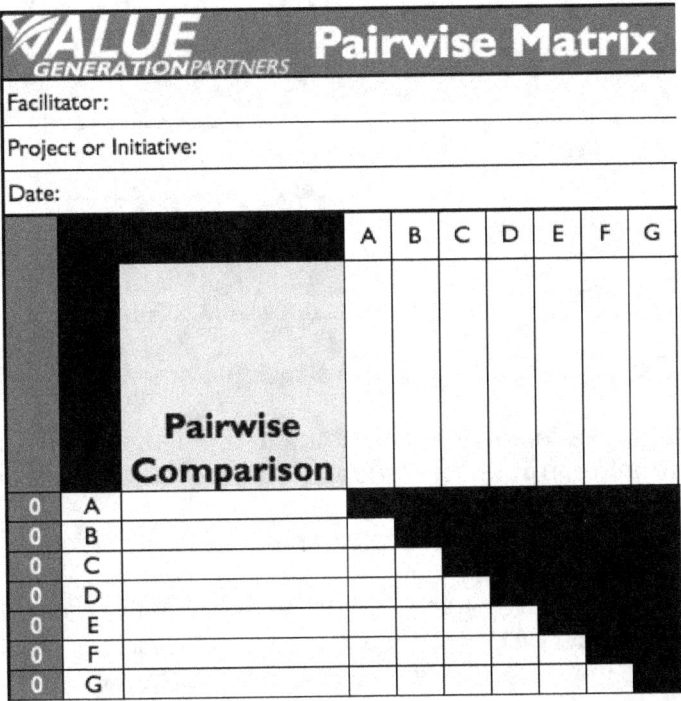

An example of using pairwise comparison is a workshop team working with the sponsor to prioritize seven project deliverables. The team lists the project deliverables from "A" to "G" on both axes of the pairwise comparison matrix. Using the matrix, each deliverable is compared in pairs. (Example: Compare deliverable A to deliverable B, then deliverable A to deliverable C, etc.) During the comparison process, the sponsor determines which is the most important deliverable in the pair, and its letter is placed in the corresponding cell. At the end of the comparison, the deliverables are ranked for priority by the number of times a deliverable's representative letter is used.

Process Maps

W. Edwards Deming is credited with the phrase, "If you can't describe what you are doing as a process, you don't know what you're doing." A process can be defined as any activity or group of activities that transforms inputs by adding value and providing an output to an internal or external customer. Process maps are the tools used to visually describe what you are doing and how you are doing it.

Inputs	Transformation	Outputs
People Equipment Environment Procedures Materials	Process	Product or Service

Process maps are made up of the following elements:

- **Inputs** are variables that contribute to or influence a process step
- **Controllable Inputs** are variables that can easily be changed to measure the effect on an output
- **Critical Inputs** are variables that have been statistically proven to effect one or more of the outputs
- **Noise Input** are variables that are very difficult to control
- **Value Added (VA)** is a process step that transforms the product or service in a way that adds value to the customer
- **Non-Value Added (NVA)** is a process step that does not transform the product or service in a way that adds value to the customer
- **Non-Value Added but Necessary (NVAN)** is a process step that does not transform the product or service in a way that adds value to the customer, but is required, typically, due to regulatory compliance
- **Outputs** are variables that result from a particular process step

Workshop Facilitator's Toolbox

As you reflect on the elements of a process, it is important to consider that all inputs have variation, all processes include value-added and non-value-added activities, and the outputs are the sum of the variation, value-added, and non-value-added activities. A well-defined and documented process map provides a starting point for future work on the process to reduce variation and eliminate non-value-added activities.

When conducting a process-mapping session, it is advantageous to encourage team members to follow (or walk) the process. The team must then come to consensus on the process steps as the final version of the map is documented. Process maps are living documents that get updated as the process changes or improvements are implemented.

Depending on the process, there are many types of process maps from which to choose to document the steps, such as the three listed below:

1. Flowcharts and block diagrams
2. Input/output process map
3. Deployment flowcharts or swimlane maps

Below are some basic and typical symbols to use when creating flowcharts and process maps:

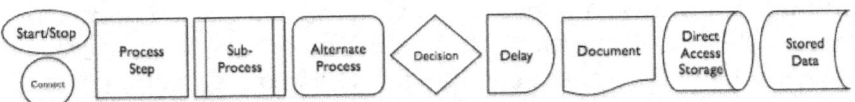

Flowcharts and block diagrams are typically used to depict simple processes with few steps. Flowcharts may be used to document process flows that do not cross multiple functions or do not require an understanding of the inputs and outputs. They may be used as a high-level view of the process or a starting point for more detailed process maps.

Workshop Facilitator's Toolbox

Flowchart or Block Diagram

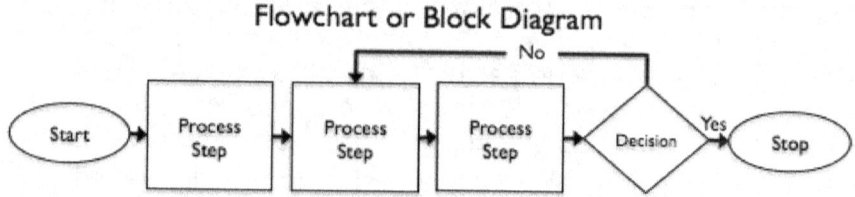

Benefits of flowcharts and block diagrams include:

- Provide a starting point for more detailed mapping
- Provide a simple and high-level visual depiction of the process flow
- Provide a consistent approach for analyzing and improving simple process flows

Process for documenting flowcharts and block diagrams:

1. Identify and document the starting point and stopping point; these are the boundaries of the process
2. Document the process steps, including any decision points, delays, documentation, etc.
3. Utilize the flowchart for the next phase of the initiative, such as to document procedures, conduct process training, or for process improvement

Input/output process maps are used to describe and understand processes with multiple steps that transform materials, services, or information into customer deliverables. These maps focus on understanding each process step, along with its associated inputs and outputs. Input/output process maps are typically used to find, understand, and correct sources of variation and to ensure the final output meets customer specifications.

Workshop Facilitator's Toolbox

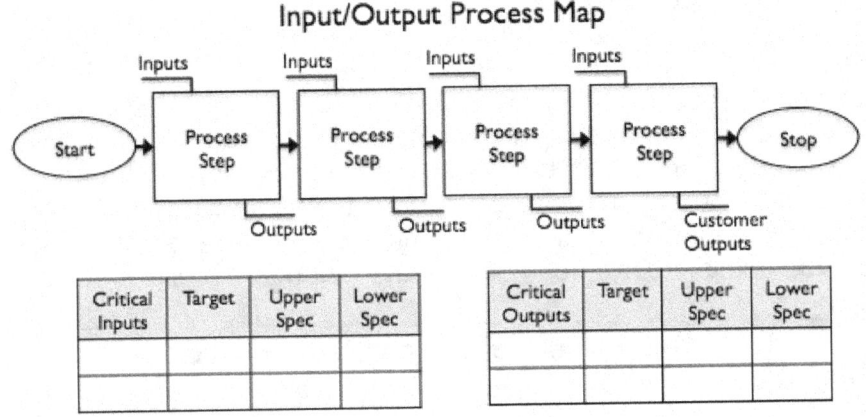

Input/Output Process Map

Benefits of input/output process maps:

- Provide a view of potential control points
- Provide a starting point for more detailed mapping
- Provide a high-level or detailed visual depiction of the process flow
- Provide a consistent approach for analyzing and improving process flows
- Provide a view of delays, decision points, non-value-added activities, and areas of variation

Process for documenting input/output process maps:

1. Identify and document the starting point and stopping point; these are the boundaries of the process
2. Document the key process steps, including any decision points, delays, documentation, etc.
3. Document inputs for each process step
4. Document outputs for each process step
5. Identify critical outputs for each process step and customer
6. Identify critical inputs for each process step
7. Add targets and operating specification for critical inputs and outputs
8. Utilize the process map for the next phase of the initiative, such as to document procedures, conduct process training, or for

Workshop Facilitator's Toolbox

process improvement

Deployment flowcharts or swimlane maps are used to understand and depict processes in situations when information, materials, and services flow with handoffs across multiple functions. These maps are typically used to find, understand, and correct sources of non-value-added waste in transactional or business processes. Creating a deployment flowchart, it becomes clear where there are handoffs, decision points, delays, loop backs, and redundant process steps.

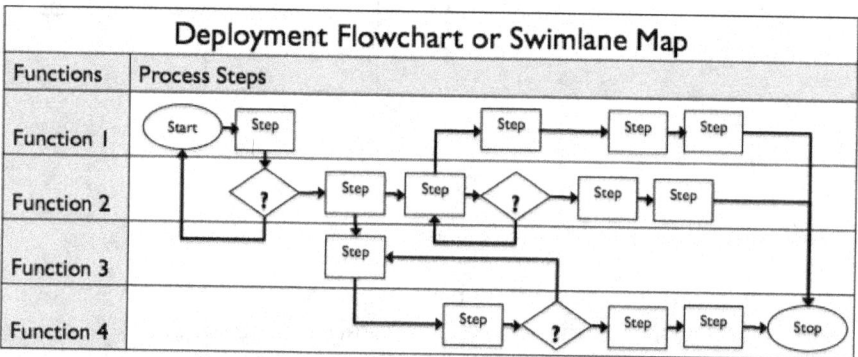

Benefits of deployment flowcharts or swimlane process maps:

- Provide a starting point for more detailed mapping
- Provide a high-level or detailed visual depiction of transactional or business processes
- Provide a consistent approach for analyzing, transactional, or business process flows
- Provide a view of non-value-added activities, such as handoffs, decision points, delays, loop backs, and redundant process steps

Process for documenting deployment flowcharts or swimlane process maps:

1. Identify and document the starting point and stopping point; they are the boundaries of the process
2. Define and document the key function or department names for each swimlane represented by the process
3. Document the flow as process steps, handoffs, decision points, and loop backs through various swimlanes
4. Utilize the process map for the next phase of the initiative, such

as to document procedures, conduct process training, or for process improvement

Any of the referenced flow charts and process maps may be used as inputs to other tools and efforts, such as:

- Cause-and-effect diagram
- Cause-and-effect matrix
- Training plan
- Control plan
- Work instructions or procedures
- Improvement workshops and initiatives

Pugh Matrix

A Pugh matrix is a selection tool used to help choose between multiple concepts for a new process, product, or service. It was originally used to evaluate and select between several product or process designs, as ranked against customer criteria and the current baseline design. Pugh matrix, also known as Pugh method and Pugh concept selection, was developed by Stuart Pugh and published in <u>Total Design</u> in 1991. While a Pugh matrix is typically used to select the best alternative among product or process designs, it may also be used to define a hybrid solution, using the best characteristics from several alternative concepts. Pugh may also be used as an alternative to the solution-selection matrix for choosing the best solution for a problem-solving project.

A Pugh matrix may be used when:

- The current process, product, or service requires redesign or improvement
- The current design is not meeting customer requirements or performing as required
- Choosing the best concept or a combination of the best characteristics among several concepts

Benefits of a Pugh matrix include:

- Reduce emotion and bias from the decision-making process
- Provide a consistent approach for selecting among several

Workshop Facilitator's Toolbox

concepts
- Provide a tool to define a hybrid design or solution based on the best characteristics from several options
- Save cost and time by efficiently and effectively selecting the best design for a new process, product, or service

Pugh Matrix Process:

1. Draw a Pugh matrix on a board or flipchart, or project an electronic matrix on a screen
2. Enter into the matrix the current design as the baseline for comparative ranking among the concepts
3. List or brainstorm optional concept designs determined to meet the voice-of-the-customer and voice-of-the-business needs for a new process, product, or service
4. List or brainstorm key criteria from which to evaluate concept options; key criteria may include critical-to-customer, critical-to-business, critical-to-quality, and critical design characteristics
5. Determine a weighting factor for each of the key criteria; weights may be determined using pairwise comparison or simply ranking on a scale of 1 to 5
6. Evaluate each concept against the current baseline design for each criterion and provide a score of +1 for better than, 0 for same as, or -1 for worse than the current baseline design
7. Sum the positive, negative, and total scores for each concept; note that the matrix template performs the calculations
8. Determine the weighted total score by multiplying each criterion weight times the individual concept score, then summing the total for each concept; note that the matrix template performs the calculations
9. Use the highest (positive) scores to determine which design concept or combination of design criterion characteristics from each concept to carry forward to the next phase of the decision or development process

An example of using a Pugh matrix is when a design team is tasked to develop a next generation smart phone. The team lists the current smart phone design as the baseline, and brainstorms four new design concepts to include in the evaluation matrix. The key design characteristics are listed in the matrix as the evaluation criterion, and each of the four design concepts are evaluated against the baseline to determine if the concept is better than, equal to, or worse than the baseline for each criterion. The concept with the best (highest, positive) score, as measured against the baseline, is used for the next design phase of the new smart phone.

The following image depicts a basic Pugh matrix template, along with its elements.

VALUE GENERATIONPARTNERS — **Pugh Matrix**

Workshop Name:							
Workshop Facilitator:							
Date:							
			Concepts				
Key Criteria		Baseline	Concept 1	Concept 2	Concept 3	Concept 4	Weight
Criterion 1		0					
Criterion 2		0					
Criterion 3		0					
Criterion 4		0					
Criterion 5		0					
Criterion 6		0					
Sum of Positives (+)		0					
Sum of Negatives (-)		0					
Overall Total		0	0	0	0	0	
Weighted Total		0	0	0	0	0	

RACI

RACI is a role-assignment matrix that helps to clarify and define the roles and assignments for large complex projects, cross-functional processes, and cross-departmental initiatives. It is a powerful tool used to depict roles – **R**esponsible, **A**ccountable, **C**onsulted, or **I**nformed – for each activity.

The role – such as workshop facilitator, sponsor, etc., rather than the person – is listed on the RACI matrix and then correlated to the assignment type, as follows:

Workshop Facilitator's Toolbox

- **R**esponsible is the role assigned to complete the activity
- **A**ccountable is the role with approval authority to make decisions and delegate responsibility of the activity; the role identified as accountable is also responsible for the completion of the activity, if no other role is assigned as **R**esponsible in the RACI matrix; this is the only case when a role may be assigned to more than one assignment type
- **C**onsulted is the role that is typically assigned to a subject matter expert (SME) who provides input, advice, and two-way communication regarding the activities
- **I**nformed is the role that is kept updated through one-way communication on progress and completion of activities

A RACI matrix may be used when:

- Activities span several departments or functions
- Initiative is large and complex, with many roles and activities
- Effort or work is cross-functional in nature
- Work is performed across several businesses, customers, or suppliers

Benefits of a RACI matrix include:

- Provide clarification on roles and assignment types
- Provide a consistent approach for role assignment
- Provide a collaborative team environment
- Provide an approach for efficiently and effectively communicating role assignments

RACI Matrix Process:

1. List roles across the top axis of the RACI matrix
2. Add activities along the side axis of the RACI matrix
3. Correlate roles and activities by adding an assignment type (i.e.: **R**esponsible, **A**ccountable, **C**onsulted, or **I**nformed)
4. Communicate RACI matrix role assignments, as appropriate and necessary

Workshop Facilitator's Toolbox

The following image depicts a basic RACI matrix template, along with its elements.

VALUE GENERATIONPARTNERS — **RACI Matrix**					
Workshop Name:					
Workshop Facilitator:					
Date:					
Responsible - Accountable - Consulted - Informed					
	Role	Role	Role	Role	Role
Activity					
Activity					
Activity					
Activity					
Activity					
Activity					
Activity					

SIPOC

SIPOC is a document summarizing high-level process, including **S**uppliers, **I**nputs, **P**rocess, **O**utputs and **C**ustomers. It is an essential tool for any operational excellence, continuous improvement, or transformation initiative. A completed SIPOC includes a list of the suppliers to the process, inputs to the process, the process itself, outputs of the process, and a list of customers of the process. Included in my SIPOC template is an additional column, titled "CTC," or Critical-To-Customer; it contains a list of the critical-to-customer characteristics expected *from* the process *by* the customer *of* the process.

A SIPOC may be useful when:

- A process is being analyzed as part of a transformation or improvement workshop
- Team members are not familiar with the process and its elements
- Process documentation is outdated or it is necessary to define a new process
- Procedures, work instructions, and/or training materials are being

Workshop Facilitator's Toolbox

developed

Benefits of a SIPOC include:

- Provide input for training materials and process documentation
- Provide a starting point for process improvement or transformation
- Provide a consistent approach for analyzing and improving a process
- Provide a simple and high-level view of the process and its elements
- Provide a collaborative team environment

SIPOC Documentation Process:

1. Draw the SIPOC diagram or project the electronic template on a screen
2. Define the high-level process (beginning to end) in a few steps as a vertical block diagram in the process section of the SIPOC; the order in which the columns of the SIPOC template are completed may vary depending on the team and the facilitator
3. Document the outputs from the process including materials, services, and information
4. Document the internal and external customers that receive the outputs of the process (customers may also be suppliers)
5. Document the inputs to the process including materials, services, and information
6. Document the internal and external suppliers of the inputs to the process (suppliers may also be customers)
7. Added to the traditional SIPOC, you may wish to document the critical-to-customer (CTC) characteristics expected from the process; the CTCs must be verified with customers of the process

The following image depicts a basic SIPOC template, along with its elements.

SIPOC

Project Name:			Project Manager:		Date:	
Suppliers	Inputs	Process	Outputs	Customers	CTCs	

Six Thinking Hats

As a facilitator, leading teams and individuals in the thinking process is key to workshop success. Edward de Bono is the author of Six Thinking Hats, a book that defines an approach for teams to conduct parallel thinking, thereby promoting focus, creativity, and productive participation. It is based on six metaphorical hats of specific color and purpose, which may be worn – metaphorically – to direct thoughts, using a process, in order to achieve a desired outcome.

By leading a team through the process of wearing and switching between six hats, the team becomes much more cohesive and productive than if left to random-thinking processes. Parallel thinking indicates that all participants "wear" the same color hat at the same time.

Thinking approach and focus by hat color:

- **Black** – considers decisions and reasoning with careful understanding of risks
- **Blue** – focuses on ensuring the thinking process is followed through action and structure
- **Green** – uses creativity and innovation to generate new ideas and alternatives
- **Red** – emotional and intuitive approach of ideation based on instinct
- **White** – emphasizes factual understanding through data and information
- **Yellow** – optimistic approach to finding value and benefits from an outcome

Workshop Facilitator's Toolbox

Benefits of Six Thinking Hats include:

- Generate innovative ideas and solutions
- Provide a collaborative team environment
- Determine value while mitigating risks
- Increase focus on goals and outcomes
- Provide structure for team dynamics and thinking
- Provide a consistent approach for generating and evaluating ideas
- Provide an approach for effectively thinking as a team

Below is an example of using Six Thinking Hats to make a decision to lease, buy, or build.

A team is facilitated using Six Thinking Hats to make a decision (lease, buy, or build) for expansion of a warehouse facility. The facilitator, being well versed on the Six Thinking Hats technique, uses the blue *process* hat to manage the session, setting the tone and direction. If the thought process drifts from intended topic and style, the facilitator applies blue hat thinking to pull back and redirect the team.

The facilitator proceeds with green *creative* hat thinking to brainstorm various alternatives associated with any of the three choices (lease, buy, or build). Brainstorming elements include warehouse location alternatives, square footage needed, types of storage and shelving, docking needs, etc. There are moments of red *emotional* hat thinking by some participants; they become passionate about the aesthetics of the building when considering an older, leased building versus a new building. While these are important considerations, the facilitator pauses the discussions for a blue hat moment to refocus, and includes aesthetics into the brainstorming considerations.

The team switches to white *fact* hat thinking, reviewing and analyzing data and information relevant to the decision. The team reviews short-term and long-term costs of leasing, buying, or building. Members determine when each option would be available to occupy and consider the implications of such on their customers' needs. Revenue, gross margins, net profits, and cash flows are calculated based on move-in dates of each option. Impacts to the workforce are evaluated and discussed.

Workshop Facilitator's Toolbox

The facilitator switches to yellow *optimism* hat thinking to define the potential value and benefits resulting from green hat brainstorming and white hat data analysis. Then, using black *risk* hat thinking, the team determines potential pitfalls and mitigations from selecting any of the alternatives.

By using a Six Thinking Hat approach, the team considers three alternatives in a structured, factual, emotional, risk, creative, and beneficial perspective. The team conducts a presentation of the process and results to leadership, gaining full support for the decision to buy an existing building for their warehouse needs.

While facilitating a team or group, it may be helpful to consider these tools, as listed below, to assist when using specific hat colors:

- **Black** – fault tree analysis, FMEA, control plan
- **Blue** – action plan, SMART goals, ground rules
- **Green** – brainstorming, nominal group technique, Pugh matrix
- **Red** – force field analysis, mind mapping, pairwise comparison, brainstorming, nominal group technique
- **White** – data analysis tools, graphical analysis tools
- **Yellow** – impact/effort matrix, decision tree, cause-and-effect diagram

Solution-Selection Matrix

A solution-selection matrix is a powerful selection tool used to choose between multiple solution alternatives during a workshop. A solution-selection matrix may also be used as an alternative to a Pugh matrix for choosing the best design concept for a new process, product, or service.

A solution-selection matrix may be used when:

- The current process has problems, issues, errors, or defects
- The current process, product, or service requires improvement
- Choosing the best solution among several potential solutions
- The current solution is not meeting customer requirements or performing as required

Workshop Facilitator's Toolbox

Benefits of a solution-selection matrix include:

- Reduce emotion and bias from the decision-making process
- Provide a consistent approach for selecting the best solution among several options
- Save cost and time by efficiently and effectively selecting the best solution
- Provide a collaborative team environment

Solution-Selection Matrix Process:

1. Draw a solution-selection matrix on a board or flipchart, or project an electronic matrix on a screen
2. List or brainstorm potential solutions to eliminate the current problems or issues
3. List or brainstorm selection criteria to evaluate potential solutions; the selection criteria may be determined with input from the sponsor
4. Determine a weight factor for each of the selection criteria; weights may be determined using pairwise comparison or simply ranking on a scale of 1 to 5
5. Evaluate each potential solution against the criteria, and enter a rank of 1 if the solution "does not meet" the criteria, 5 for "somewhat meets" the criteria, or 9 for "fully meets" the criteria
6. Determine the weighted score by multiplying each selection criteria weight by the individual solution score, then summing the total for each concept; note that the matrix template performs these calculations
7. Determine which solution(s) to implement in order to eliminate issues and problems with the current solution or process

An example using a solution-selection matrix is a continuous improvement team analyzing several potential solutions to reduce defects found during testing at a software development company. The team analyzes the process and the causes of the defects, and then develops a list of eight potential solutions to prevent the defects. The potential solutions are evaluated against the selection criteria listed in the matrix; those potential solutions with the highest scores are selected for implementation.

Workshop Facilitator's Toolbox

The following image depicts a basic solution-selection matrix template, along with its elements.

VALUE GENERATIONPARTNERS		**Solution-Selection Matrix**									
Facilitator:									Date:		
Goal Statement:											
Root Cause Statement:											
							Selection Criteria				
				Low Effort	High Impact	Acceptable Cost	Acceptable Time	Acceptable Risk	Resources Available	Cultural Acceptance	Addresses Root Cause
			Weight								
Output (y) or CTC	Root Cause (x)	Potential Solution	(1=No, 5=Somewhat, 9=Yes)							Total Score	Implement (Y or N)
										0	
										0	
										0	
										0	
										0	
										0	
										0	

SWOT Analysis

SWOT Analysis is a great tool to determine the **S**trengths, **W**eaknesses, **O**pportunities, and **T**hreats of a business, strategy, service, product, project, department, or a function! SWOT is often credited to Albert Humphrey of Stanford University, when, in the 1960s and 1970s, he led research projects using data from many top companies.

SWOT analysis can be performed as a transformational effort, a strategic planning tool, or a precursor to cultural change for every type of entity or topic. It can be beneficial when performed as a proactive event to determine directional corrections prior to a change implementation or as a reactive session to determine changes to improve an existing situation.

A SWOT analysis identifies internal characteristics and external elements that are significant to influencing or achieving a desired outcome of the SWOT topic. The SWOT analysis matrix is divided

Workshop Facilitator's Toolbox

into two categories (Internal and External) and four elements (Strengths, Weaknesses, Opportunities, and Threats).

Internal categories are *strengths* and *weaknesses*
- **Strengths** are internal characteristics that will drive achievement of the desired outcome
- **Weaknesses** are internal characteristics that may prevent the desired outcome, if not reinforced

External elements are *opportunities* and *threats*
- **Opportunities** are external elements that can be leveraged to achieve the desired outcome
- **Threats** are external elements that may prevent achieving the desired outcome, if not mitigated

A SWOT analysis may be used as:

- Input to transformational or operational excellence initiatives
- A determination of initiative, program, or project viability
- A precursor to strategic planning
- A team approach tool for defining input to programs and projects

Benefits of SWOT analysis include:

- Provide valuable input for strategic planning initiatives, programs, and projects
- Proactive approach to determine which initiatives, programs, and projects to undertake
- Provide input for developing an action plan and assigning resources
- Provide a collaborative team environment
- Bring together diverse backgrounds and experiences

Follow the steps below for a simple approach to conduct a SWOT analysis:

1. Describe and document the reason, objective, and intended outcome for performing an analysis on the SWOT topic
2. Conduct the SWOT analysis by brainstorming a list of internal characteristics and external elements related to the situation or desired outcome
3. Prioritize the list – by category and element – for actions to

leverage, mitigate, overcome, or exploit
   a. Map the strengths to opportunities, which can be leveraged, and to threats, which can be mitigated
   b. Understand weaknesses that need to be overcome to take advantage of opportunities, and that might be exploited by threats
4. Develop an action plan describing "who, what, and when," based on the prioritization you did in the previous step

An example of using SWOT analysis is a cross-functional team at a medium-sized retail clothing chain, working on its clothing lines and floor layouts for the new shopping season. The team uses the SWOT analysis to understand its internal strengths and weaknesses with its current offerings and store layouts, as well as its external opportunities and threats based on consumer buying trends, competitor offerings, and competitor store designs. Using the SWOT information, the team designs new store layouts and defines a plan for clothing lines to offer during the upcoming season.

The following image depicts a basic SWOT analysis template, along with its elements.

VALUE GENERATION PARTNERS — SWOT Analysis

Facilitator:		Date:	
SWOT Topic:			
Internal Strengths	**Score**	**Internal Weaknesses**	**Score**
External Opportunities	**Score**	**External Threats**	**Score**

Workshop Facilitator's Toolbox

Team Building

Henry Ford, the founder of Ford Motor Company, delivered a clear and concise message regarding the importance of teams and the power of team building by saying, "Coming together is a beginning. Keeping together is progress. Working together is success." A team consists of people with complementary skills who are committed to a common purpose, with action plans and a set of performance goals for which it takes ownership and holds itself accountable. The strength and success of an organization's workshops is highly dependent on a strong team culture.

American industrialist and philanthropist Andrew Carnegie once said, "Teamwork is the ability to work together toward a common vision – the ability to direct individual accomplishments toward organizational objectives. It is the fuel that allows common people to attain uncommon results." Recognizing, understanding, and building on the stages of team development are critical to successfully conducting workshops. Psychologist Bruce Tuckman used the phrase "forming, storming, norming, and performing" in the article, <u>Development Sequence in Small Groups</u>, in 1965, to describe the process of group development in achieving high performance and delivering results.

Below are the four stages of team development:

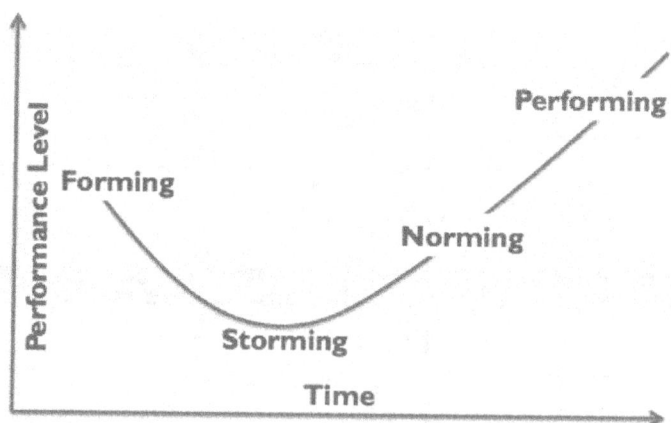

Forming – members are typically excited, anxious, positive, and polite

- Have a strong dependency on the facilitator
- Starting to work together and get to know each other
- Feeling uncertain about their roles within the team
- Not yet sure what is expected of them nor what they may contribute
- Beginning to understand goals, deliverables, processes, and procedures

As a workshop facilitator of a team in the **forming** stage, your role is to provide clear and concise goals, objectives, and deliverables, and to provide the team with direction on roles and responsibilities. Encourage team members to have open dialogue and help members settle into their new assignments.

Storming – members begin to think individually, have conflict, are distracted from the goals

- Loyalties are divided; leadership is challenged
- Teams engage in confrontation, disagreements, arguments, complaining
- Split into sub-groups due to lack of trust for other members and/or leader
- Question the approach, methods, processes being used
- Challenge support for the team; may begin to rebel

As a workshop facilitator of a team in the **storming** stage, it is necessary to take on a more directive role in order to establish structure, clearly define how the team will work together, and clarify roles and responsibilities. It is your responsibility to build trust, resolve conflict, address concerns, and provide resolutions amenable to all members. You must recognize and address when members revisit the storming stage, typically due to membership changes, goals changing, or leadership changes.

Norming – members start working together, have less conflict, focus on the goals

- Goals, deliverables, and approach are understood and supported

Workshop Facilitator's Toolbox

by members
- Understand and accept their roles and responsibilities, as well as others' roles and responsibilities
- Begin to work together as a cohesive team; trust and collaboration exist
- Focus is switched from conflict and challenge to achieving goals

As a workshop facilitator of a team in the **norming** stage, your role is to coordinate the team's functions and activities at a high level, and to guide the team to take responsibility and manage toward the goal.

Performing – members begin to focus on the process, operate efficiently, achieve goals

- Trust, positive energy, motivation, enthusiasm
- Ownership and clarity of the goals, approach, activities, tasks
- Exhibit open dialogue and communications
- Knowledgeable, competent, able to manage decision-making process
- Rely on each other; collaborative, interdependent cooperation
- Handle conflict; reach consensus

As a workshop facilitator of a team in the **performing** stage, your role is to delegate much of the authority and decision making to the team; focus your efforts on developing team members.

Benefits of building effective teams include:

- Environment of skill development and learning
- Approach for personal growth and satisfaction
- Collaborative environment; sense of belonging
- Environment where silos and barriers do not exist
- Inclusive understanding of the organization
- Environment to efficiently and effectively resolve issues that individuals alone cannot resolve
- Diverse and inclusive environment in which individuals work toward common goals

Characteristics of a *successful* team include members having:

- An understanding of their roles and responsibilities

Workshop Facilitator's Toolbox

- An understanding of their purpose and goals, as well as a documented plan for how to achieve those goals
- Participation in team discussions and decisions, and to share accountability and ownership of execution and results
- Respect for each other and a commitment to resolve conflicts
- Appropriate communication and listening skills
- A use of fact-based decision making with data and statistical analysis
- Effective and efficient meetings, with adherence to ground rules and suitable record keeping

Workshop Facilitator's contribution to a team's success includes:

- Provide sense of purpose and mission
- Provide plan and goals with direction and support
- Share business results
- Reinforce positive outcomes

Characteristics of an *ineffective* team include:

- Unclear goals and objectives, with no plan or little documentation
- Unclear roles and responsibilities
- Dominating members force their ideas on others
- Members' ideas are ignored and actions are limited
- Lack of involvement and communication
- Making decisions on instinctive reaction, with no facts or data to support
- Blame, unresolved conflict, lack of trust
- Tangents, digression, lack of focus

Team Building Process:

1. Determine the type of team required, based on the goals and objectives
2. Assemble and launch the team
3. Conduct reviews to identify the team's stage of development
4. Determine appropriate actions to move the team to performing stage
5. Take action with team until performing stage is achieved
6. Once team's goals are achieved, adjourn the team and celebrate its success

Training Plan

Most workshops result in a new process, product, or service, which require some amount and level of training. In today's global and fast-paced environment, it is difficult to find time to conduct training sessions, so the necessary training may be delivered in the several methods:

- **eLearning** – participants take the training via computer at their own pace and time
- **Instructor-led** – participants attend an in-class session that is facilitated by an instructor
- **Virtual** – participants dial-in and logon to a web-based training session that is led by a remote instructor
- **Blended learning** – participants may take the training in a combination of instructor-led, virtual, and/or eLearning sessions

A training plan is useful when:

- A workshop results in a new process, product, or service
- A workshop crosses many functions or departments
- The workshop impacts safety, quality, or customer service

Benefits of developing a training plan include:

- Provide a consistent approach for analyzing, developing, delivering, and validating training
- Provide an approach for efficiently and effectively executing training
- Provide a collaborative team environment
- Save cost and time by developing and delivering training appropriate to the project

Training Plan Process:

1. Training topic is identified as part of the workshop deliverables
2. A training needs analysis and materials design/development owner is identified and assigned
3. Trainer is identified and assigned
4. Training logistics – including participants, delivery date, training duration, and delivery method – are determined and defined

Workshop Facilitator's Toolbox

5. Training is delivered, evaluated, and adjusted
6. Training results are validated to ensure the training intent was achieved

The following image depicts a basic training plan template, along with its elements.

VALUE GENERATION PARTNERS	Training Management Plan							
Workshop Facilitator:				Date:				
Workshop Solution:								
Analyze - Design - Develop				Deliver - Evaluate - Adjust - Validate				
Who	What	When	Other	Who		When	How	Other
Owner	Topic	Due Date	Status Comments	Trainer	Participant(s)	Date	Duration	Method	Results Comments

Summary: Workshop Facilitation for Success

Workshop Facilitation for Success is an efficient and effective approach to managing and achieving goals and objectives in a face-to-face, cross-functional environment. Workshop facilitation (also known as Kaizen events, continuous improvement events, quality improvement events, workout sessions, and process improvement events) may be conducted as one-day to five-day events. Workshops are conducted to achieve goals and objectives based on many purposes, such as process improvement, waste reduction, cost-of-quality reduction, project selection, and strategy development and deployment. Much thought and consideration must be given to planning and conducting workshop facilitation to ensure successful outcomes.

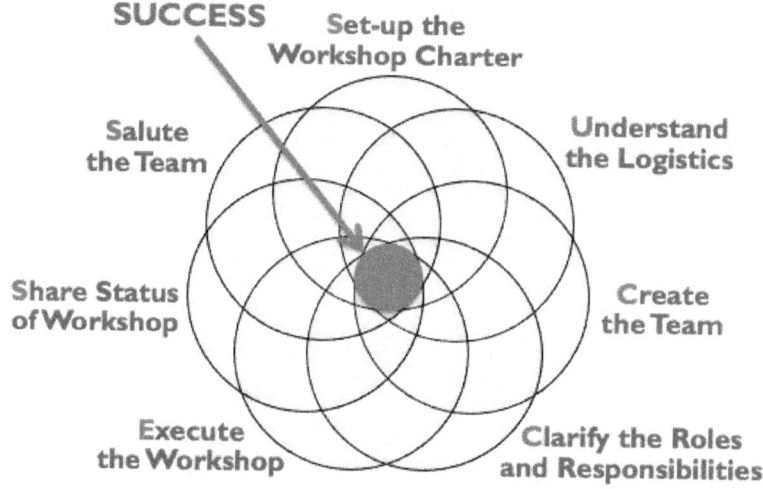

This simple seven-step approach, called Workshop Facilitation for Success, may be applied to achieve goals and objectives in any industry – healthcare, construction, manufacturing, service, hospitality, non-profit, government, financial, etc. Workshop Facilitation for Success is designed for facilitators of all levels, regardless of their role, business, and industry. It combines the most effective and efficient elements of workshop facilitation approaches into the following seven steps:

1. Set-up the Workshop Charter

Summary: Workshop Facilitation for Success

2. Understand the Logistics
3. Create the Team
4. Clarify Roles and Responsibilities
5. Execute the Workshop
6. Share Status of Workshop
7. Salute the Team

Workshop facilitation may be useful when:

- There are many and varying opinions on how to achieve goals and objectives
- Goals and objectives must be completed in a short cycle time
- Team and cross-functional collaboration are necessary to ensure success of goals and objectives
- It is necessary for a group to work in a face-to-face environment to achieve goals and objectives
- Goals and objectives include waste reduction, cycle-time reduction, process improvement, or quality improvement

Benefits of workshop facilitation include:

- Provide a collaborative team environment
- Provide a consistent approach for facilitating workshops
- Increase focus and attention on goals and objectives
- Save cost and time through rapid goal and objective achievement
- Provide an efficient and effective approach for achieving goals and objectives

We wish you much success in your pursuit of Workshop Facilitation for Success, thereby generating greater organizational value!

www.ingramcontent.com/pod-product-compliance
Lightning Source LLC
Chambersburg PA
CBHW070303220526
45465CB00004B/1723